NTC's Language Project Books

De tous côtés 1

National Textbook Company

a division of NTC/CONTEMPORARY PUBLISHING GROUP, INC.
Lincolnwood, Illinois USA

Development and Production: Elm Street Publications, Wellesley, MA
Composition: Jan Ewing, Ewing Systems, New York, NY
Illustrations: Len Shalansky
Electronic Art: William J. Cataldi, Ewing Systems, New York, NY

ISBN: 0-658-00310-0 (hardbound)
ISBN: 0-658-00093-4 (softbound)

Published by National Textbook Company,
a division of NTC/Contemporary Publishing Group, Inc.
4255 West Touhy Avenue
Lincolnwood (Chicago), Illinois 60646-1975 U.S.A.
© 2000 NTC/Contemporary Publishing Group, Inc.

Manufactured in the United States of America.

99 00 01 02 03 04 05 QB 9 8 7 6 5 4 3 2 1

Table des Matières

To the Student

You are studying a foreign language—French. And languages are meant to be spoken. But people talk for a reason: maybe to tell a friend about something that's just happened, or to ask about the time a movie starts. Well, **De tous côtés 1** also provides reasons for using language—different situations in which you need to speak, read, and write French.

De tous côtés 1 consists of ten projects that relate to topics ordinarily taught in first-year French. You may do them in the order that fits your textbook. Why projects? Because each one has a different goal and includes a different reason for using French. Because you'll have the satisfaction of actually using French to create something. Some of the projects involve:

- Setting up and going to a restaurant typical of a French-speaking area

- Planning mini-Olympic games for the French-speaking world

- Creating a French-language weather report

- Producing a French-language fashion show

- Setting up a health clinic for French-speaking clients

- Making a holiday calendar for the French-speaking world

You'll reach the goals of these projects in many different ways. To make a calendar, for example, you'll research holidays in French-speaking countries and regions. That research could be done on the World Wide Web, if you have access to it. Once on the Web, you can search for information in both French and English! To give a weather report, you'll need to change Fahrenheit temperatures into Celsius because after all, that's what people from most French-speaking countries and regions use and understand.

A resource section of special tools is available in the Almanac in the back of **De tous côtés 1**. It contains lots of helpful information, including the following:

- A list of the French-speaking countries and regions with their capitals and a monetary unit chart with directions for changing money from dollars to the currencies of various French-speaking countries

- A guide for doing searches on the World Wide Web

- Extra vocabulary related to the projects you're working on

- A metric chart with directions for converting standard U.S. measurements

De tous côtés 1 includes other features to help you. Each project begins with a list of the tasks to be performed. This is a kind of road map showing what you can accomplish. There is even a **Connexions** (*Connections*) box indicating other subject areas related to this project, such as history, art, technology, or study skills. The **Ressources utiles** (*Useful resources*) boxes suggest sources for finding information you will need, as well as materials required for each step in the project. This may include worksheets to help you organize and present infor- mation. Worksheets are available from your teacher, and activities that use them have a worksheet icon in the margin of the text. The **Vocabulaire** (*Vocabulary*) boxes include French words and phrases you may need to complete a step in the project.

While you're working through a project, you'll see interesting tidbits of information about French-speaking countries and regions in the **Saviez-vous que ... ?** (*Did you know that ... ?*) boxes. They present interesting facts, such as why French students place pictures of fish on each oth- ers' backs on April Fools' Day, and how to say *bell bottoms* in French.

During a project, you will often work with partners or a small group of other students. In Project 6, **Présentez votre lyceé**, you might make classroom signs, or perhaps videotape important areas of the school for the student guidebook. Occasionally you'll work on your own. You may see an icon indicating that a task can be done as homework.

While you work with other students on these projects, you will have many opportunities to speak, read, and write French. You may play the role of an exchange student, talk with your host, and later write a thank-you note in French. In Project 4, you will play a game that a group has invented. You may have to read and answer questions in French.

But what if you'd like to add something extra to a project? Maybe you'd like a challenge. In each project, **Un peu plus** (*Something extra*) sections provide those opportunities. You can spread your wings and push your French to its limits.

In these projects, French is everywhere; it is necessary and useful. You and your classmates will have the satisfaction of using French in real-life situations and enjoying it.

Amuse-toi bien!

Faisons connaissance

For this project, your class will plan a visit to a French-speaking country or region. You will be working in one of two groups. One group will consist of students from the U.S. who are "visiting" a major city in a French-speaking country or region. The other group will be the host students. During the course of this project, you will:

- Decide on a city in a French-speaking country or region to visit
- Write a letter of introduction to one of the new students you're going to meet
- Find the best flight times and fares to your destination (visitors)
- Find ways to pick up your guests at the airport and create a welcome banner (hosts)
- Introduce yourself personally to the new students
- Investigate a site for a group excursion and design postcards from the site
- Write a note to a new friend

Bon voyage!

Connexions

As you explore a new city and meet new people, you'll sharpen your skills in many areas.

- ✔ Art
- ✔ Géographie
- ✔ Histoire
- ✔ Mathématiques
- ☐ Médias

- ☐ Musique
- ☐ Santé et nutrition
- ☐ Sciences
- ✔ Stratégies d'étude
- ✔ Technologie

Look for the **Connexions** boxes throughout this project.

Warm-up: Bonjour!

Ressources utiles

■ A three-ring binder or folder for each student for compiling a portfolio

---

A. With two or three other students, create a list of words and phrases in French that you associate with greetings and introductions. Share your ideas with your class and expand your list as you listen to your classmates' ideas. How are French greetings and introductions similar to or different from greetings and introductions in the U.S.?

B. In a group of three or four, discuss what greetings and introductions in the U.S. are like. What are the typical words and phrases people say when meeting someone new? Do people shake hands? How might greetings between two friends be different from those between two business associates?

Hi!   Hey!   How are you?

How do you do?

Hello!   Howdy!   Mornin'!

It's a pleasure to meet you.

Good morning!

c. As you plan and carry out your trip, you'll be putting together a portfolio of your experiences and accomplishments. You'll need a three-ring binder. Begin your portfolio by inserting the list of words and phrases you and your classmates brainstormed. You may want to refer to this list throughout the project.

Les préparatifs

There are over fifty French-speaking, or Francophone, countries and regions. Each has its own distinct geography, attractions, history, and culture. After researching various possibilities, your class will decide on one city to visit on your exchange trip.

Ressources utiles

- World map
- World Map Worksheet 1.A, pages 1 and 2
- Colored markers
- Maps of French-speaking countries and regions
- Encyclopedias
- Guidebooks for French-speaking countries
- Travel magazines or brochures with photographs of French-speaking cities
- TV programs about selected cities
- Portfolio
- The World Wide Web

1ʳᵉ Étape ## Le monde francophone

A. Working in a group of three or four students, see how many French-speaking countries and regions you can name. When you're done, share your list with the class and make a complete list together on the board. Compare your list with the one in the Almanac at the back of this book.

B. Continue working in your group. Each person should have a copy of World Map Worksheet 1.A. Color all the French-speaking countries and regions the same color and label each with its name. Consult your French textbook or the Almanac for help.

Connexions

- ☑ Géographie
- ☑ Stratégies d'étude
- ☑ Technologie

c. In your group, choose three French-speaking countries or regions on your map. Think of at least two things you associate with each one. Consider cities, famous people, arts, geographical landmarks, foods, climate, and so on. Record your associations on World Map Worksheet 1.A, page 2, and share them with the class.

Pays et régions	*Associations*
▶ le Québec:	1. French-speaking part of Canada
	2. Winter *Carnaval* festival
la Polynésie française:	1. Tahiti with its beautiful beaches
	2. Painter Paul Gauguin made life there look perfect.

Saviez-vous que...?

French is spoken worldwide by 200 million people, as either their first or their second language. In some places, such as Niger and Senegal, several different groups of people make up the population of the country and each group has its own language. School subjects may be taught in French and the government may publish official documents in French; French is an "administrative language" that everyone understands. Because these countries were French and Belgian colonies, business and government have always been conducted in French.

2ᵉ Étape   Quelle ville?

 Your group's next step is to learn something new about a city in a French-speaking country or region that interests you. On a map, locate a city you'd like to visit in one of the countries or regions you chose above and write its name on World Map Worksheet 1.A, page 2. Use some of the resources listed in the **Ressources utiles** box on page 6 to find out at least five facts that you didn't already know about the city. Record them on World Map Worksheet 1.A, page 2.

Explorons le Web!

Look for information about a French-speaking city via the Web. Use the Reference or Travel sections of a Web guide to link to encyclopedias and national or local travel-related sites. Be sure to keep the addresses of sites that are of particular interest. Write them down or use the Bookmark feature of your navigation software. This feature is usually accessible from one of your pull-down menus. If any of the terms used here are unfamiliar to you, you can look them up in the Web Search Guide in the Almanac at the end of this book. The Web Search Guide also contains general guidelines for searching the Web.

3ᵉ Étape   Le choix final

In English, try to persuade the rest of the class that the city you've chosen would be the best destination for a student exchange trip!

A. With your group, prepare a brief but convincing presentation for your class—in English—about your city. Use the information you've gathered and try to include some photographs of the city from guidebooks, travel brochures, magazines, or the Web. Use World Map Worksheet 1.A, page 1, to show where the country and city are located.

B. After the presentations, hold a class vote to determine which city is the class favorite. That city will be the destination of your student exchange trip! On World Map Worksheet 1.A, page 1, outline the country or region your class has chosen in a contrasting color. Add World Map Worksheet 1.A and the information that you gathered about your city to your portfolio.

4ᵉ Étape   Formez vos groupes

For much of the rest of this project, you will be working in one of two groups. One group will be the host students in the city you've chosen. The other group will be the exchange students visiting from the U.S.

Les lettres de présentation

Before the trip begins, the visitors and the hosts will want to find out something about each other. A short letter can provide a good introduction.

Ressources utiles

■ A self-portrait or a drawing of you and your family
■ Portfolio

1ʳᵉ Étape ## L'essentiel

Before you write a letter to one of the new students you're going to meet, think about how you want to introduce yourself.

A. Find a partner from your own group (host students or visiting students). In English, brainstorm a list of standard information that should be included in a letter of introduction. Then come up with a list of phrases in French that will help you express this information in your letter. Keep in mind whether you're host students or visiting students.

Standard information	Phrases
▶ *name:*	Je m'appelle ___.
hometown:	Je suis de ___.

B. Share your French phrases with the class and make a list together on the board.

Connexions

☑ Art
☑ Stratégies
    d'étude

2ᵉ Étape   L'information personnelle

Make a list of the personal information you want to include in your letter, using the topics you brainstormed in the **1ʳᵉ Étape**. If you're one of the host students, you'll need to invent a French-speaking identity: a name, address, and so on.

3ᵉ Étape   Les lettres

A. Choose an exchange partner from the other group. Write a brief letter introducing yourself to your exchange partner. Include a self-portrait or a drawing of yourself and your family. For help with the format of a French letter, see the example on the facing page and the Almanac at the back of this book.

Vocabulaire

Cher [*male name*]	Dear [*male name*]
Chère [*female name*]	Dear [*female name*]
Ton nouvel ami/Ta nouvelle amie	Your new friend
À bientôt!	See you soon!
Je n'ai pas de frères (sœurs).	I don't have any brothers (sisters).
J'aime le sport.	I like sports.
J'aime jouer au/à la/à l'/aux ___.	I like to play [*name of game*].
J'aime jouer du/de la/de l'/ des ___.	I like to play [*name of musical instrument*].

B. Give your letter to your teacher for delivery to your exchange partner. If your exchange partner is a host, put his or her real name on the back so your teacher knows whom to deliver it to. Read the letter you've received and add it to your portfolio. If you have any problems understanding your letter, consult your teacher.

Chicago, le 21 septembre

Cher Pascal,

Je m'appelle Tom. J'ai 14 ans. Je suis de Chicago,
Illinois. J'ai deux frères et un chien (c'est nous
sur la photo). J'aime jouer au tennis, lire et
nager.

À bientôt!

Tom Pollock

XXX XXXXX
XXXX XXXXXXX XXXX
XXXX, XX

M. Pascal Deschamps
127, rue de Rousselet
13007 Marseille
FRANCE

Saviez-vous que...?

The **code postal** on a French address comes before the name of the city. It is made up of five digits. The first two digits correspond to the **département** the city is in. (Metropolitan France is divided into 96 **départements**.) For example, Marseilles is in the **département** of **Les Bouches-du-Rhône,** which is **département 13,** so its **code postal** begins with **13.**

Un @ peu plus

Now see if you can find two people in your group (hosts or visitors)
who have something in common with your exchange partner. Survey at
least five classmates, sharing information from the letter you received.
Be sure to keep your notes in your portfolio so you can tell your
exchange partner later what you found out.

▶ *You:*   Mon ami Thomas a deux frères.
                   Tu as aussi deux frères?

Group member 1: Non, je n'ai pas deux frères.

Group member 2: Oui, j'ai aussi deux frères!

Le voyage

Before the exchange trip gets under way, the visitors need to make travel plans, and the hosts need to make plans to receive the visitors.

Ressources utiles

- Airline flight schedules and fares to the city you've chosen
- The World Wide Web
- Portfolio
- Markers, paper, tape
- Computer with word-processing software

1re Étape   Pour les invités: Les billets d'avion

This **Étape** is for visitors. The visitors need to research flight times and prices to make sure they find the best bargains. Work with three or four other students from your group.

A. Using the airline flight schedules and fare lists, find out what flights are available from your hometown (or the nearest airport) to the city you've selected for the exchange trip. Make a list of five different possible dates and times. Include the arrival times in the French-speaking city and record the flight numbers and the names of the airline.

B. Find out the fare for each of the flights. Use the monetary unit chart in the Almanac section of this book and exchange rates available from newspapers, banks, or the Web to list the prices in both dollars and the currency of the French-speaking country or region.

Connexions

 Art
 Mathématiques
☑ Stratégies
   d'étude
☑ Technologie

2ᵉ Étape   Pour les hôtes: L'accueil des invités

A. This **Étape** is for the hosts. Brainstorm ways of getting to the airport to pick up your guests. Choose the best way to go by taking a vote and then decide what arrangements need to be made. Do you need to rent a vehicle?

B. Now make welcome banners to greet your visitors. Be creative and try to use both French and English on them. Use some of the materials suggested in the **Ressources utiles** box on page 13. Keep the banners for later use.

BIENVENUE!

3ᵉ Étape   La décision

Each visitor reports to the class in French the date, time, and fare of one of the flights his or her group has selected. The teacher writes the information on the board, and the class then decides which flight is the best choice for the whole group.

4ᵉ Étape   L'album

Add your list of flight times and fares as well as the group's final choice of a flight to your portfolio.

Saviez-vous que...?

It's hard to find coin-operated public phones in France, as they have gradually been replaced by card-operated phones that require a **télécarte** (*phone card*). **Télécartes** are sold at post offices, **kiosques** (*newsstands*), some cafés, railroad stations, and banks. You can also purchase them at different kinds of stores that have the sign **Télécartes en vente ici** (*Telecartes sold here*).

Un peu plus

Work with your partner from the other group. Together, prepare a telephone conversation in French. If you are the visitor, call your host partner. You will need to introduce yourself, ask for your partner, and tell him or her where you're from. Then say where your group is arriving, what the flight number is, and the time and date you are coming. If you're a host, you'll need to answer the phone, greet your partner, and respond to his or her introduction. Then ask when the group will arrive and take down the information your partner gives you. You might need to ask the caller to repeat something.

Vocabulaire

Allô.	*Hello. (on telephone)*
Ici ___.	*This is ___.*
Qui est à l'appareil?	*Who's calling?*
C'est [name].	*This is ___.*
Est-ce que je peux parler à [name]?	*May I speak with ___?*
Nous venons de [name of city].	*We're coming from ___.*
À quelle heure arrivez-vous?	*What time do you get in?*
Nous arrivons à l'aéroport de [name].	*We're arriving at ___ airport.*
C'est d'accord?	*Is that good?*
Nous arrivons le [date] à [time].	*We arrive on the ___ at ___.*
On se voit à l'aéroport à [time].	*See you at the airport at ___.*

La rencontre

hen the visitors arrive in their French-speaking city, the hosts greet them at a gathering with the exchange coordinator (your teacher).

Ressources utiles

- Adhesive name tags or index cards and tape
- Markers
- Welcome banners made in Section C
- Portfolio

1re Étape   ### Je me présente ...

At this first meeting, you're going to introduce yourself to the new students. Prepare a name tag to help your new friends learn your name. In addition to your name, add one piece of information about yourself in French that will help stimulate conversation with your new friends, such as your age, whether you have siblings or pets, or the name of an activity that you really enjoy.

Vocabulaire

J'ai [14] ans.	*I'm [14] years old.*
J'ai [un frère/deux sœurs].	*I have [a brother/two sisters].*
Je n'ai pas de [frères/sœurs].	*I don't have any [brothers/sisters].*
J'ai [un chat/un chien/un poisson rouge].	*I have [a cat/a dog/a goldfish].*
J'aime [jouer au foot].	*I like [to play soccer].*
J'aime [lire les romans].	*I like [to read novels].*

Connexions

- ☑ Art
- ☑ Stratégies d'étude

2ᵉ Étape   Et toi?

Working with a partner from your group (host students or visiting students), write at least three questions in French that you want to ask your new friends when you meet.

3ᵉ Étape   Enchanté!

Now it's time to meet your new friends! Don't forget to wear your name tag and bring your questions to the introductory gathering. Hosts should be sure to hang up the welcome banners in the classroom.

A. First, find your exchange partner and introduce yourself in French. If you can't find your exchange partner, ask around.

▶ *You:*   Pardon, je cherche Vanessa. Où est-elle?
Student: Elle est là-bas.
You: Tu es Vanessa?
Vanessa: Oui, c'est moi.

B. Now introduce yourself to at least three other students. Use your list of questions and the information on their name tags to start a conversation with each of them.

Saviez-vous que...?

Greetings in France and the U.S. are somewhat different. In France, at each meeting or good-bye, close friends and family members kiss each other on the cheek. The number of kisses (two to four) depends on the geographic area where the people live. Other friends and acquaintances always shake hands.

4ᵉ Étape   L'album

Add your list of questions and your name tag to your portfolio to keep as remembrances of meeting your exchange partner for the first time.

Un peu plus

In French, introduce your exchange partner to one of the people in your group with whom he or she has something in common. Use the information from the **Un peu plus** activity in Section B on page 12. Give your friend's name and tell your exchange partner what he or she has in common with your friend.

▶ Olivier, je te présente mon amie Jennifer. Jennifer a 14 ans et elle fait du ski.

Organisez une excursion

A long with meeting new people, your exchange trip includes an excursion to a site of interest in the French-speaking city you've chosen.

Ressources utiles

- Encyclopedias
- Guidebooks for French-speaking countries and regions
- Travel brochures and magazines
- Blank 3" x 5" index cards
- Colored markers
- Portfolio
- The World Wide Web

1re Étape   Le thème

A. To help you decide what type of site you'd like to visit, choose two topics that interest you in the following list.

l'art	la technologie	la nature	les boutiques
le théâtre	l'architecture	la géographie	les sports
les ruines	la politique	la musique	l'histoire

B. Present your selections to the class and find two or three people who share your interests.

▶ *Student 1:* Est-ce que tu aimes le théâtre?
Student 2: Oui, j'aime le théâtre.
Student 3: Non, je n'aime pas le théâtre.

Connexions

☑ Art
☑ Géographie
☑ Histoire
☑ Technologie

2ᵉ Étape   La recherche

A. Now work with your group of three or four to find a site that reflects one of the areas of interest you've chosen. Use some of the resources listed in the **Ressources utiles** box on page 19. The site must be in or near the city where the exchange trip is taking place. Based on the information you find, make a list of three reasons in French why you would like to visit the site.

▶ *Topic:*   la politique

    Site: le palais de l'Élysée

    Reasons: 1. Le président habite dans ce palais.
                The president lives in this palace.

            2. Il y a une grande fête ici le quatorze juillet.
                There's a big party here on July 14.

            3. Le jardin est très beau.
                The garden is very beautiful.

Explorons le Web!

Look back at useful Web sites you located in Section A on page 8. Check for information about specific places, such as museums or monuments, that you would like to visit in your city. Once you're on the Web site, you can look for information about the places you're interested in, links to additional pages within the site, and links to other sites with information about places of interest.

What if you already know of a place in your city that you would like to know more about? Enter its name, such as "Louvre Museum," in the search function of your navigation software. If you only have a particular theme in mind, for example, historical monuments in Luxembourg, you can search via the city and theme. *Tip:* If your keyword is a phrase, put it in quotation marks. Remember not to put two words together in quotation marks unless you want to find them together as a phrase on a Web page.

Keywords

name of museum
"[name of city] +
[theme]"

B. With your small group, present your site to the class in English or French.

3e Étape — Les cartes postales

While visiting your site, you will want to buy and write some postcards to your friends back home.

A. Working with a partner from your group, design two postcards showing the site you visited. Decorate one side of an index card with an image of the site. On the other side in the upper left corner include the name and a brief description of the place in French (or in English).

B. On your postcard, write a brief message in French to send to another French class in the visiting students' school in the U.S. If you're a host student, be sure to introduce yourself.

C. Include your research and your postcard in your portfolio.

Chers amis,

Bonjour de Nice. C'est Mardi Gras. J'adore les costumes et la musique. Je n'aime pas le bruit. Je m'amuse bien. À bientôt.

Amitiés,

Karen

Chère classe,

Bonjour de Patrice. Je suis l'ami de Karen. Je suis aussi à Nice. Karen aime beaucoup le carnaval. Moi aussi. À bientôt!

Amicalement,

Patrice

Vocabulaire

Je suis à [Luxembourg].	*I'm in [Luxembourg].*
J'écris de [la Côte d'Azur].	*I'm writing from [the Riviera].*
Je m'amuse bien.	*I'm having a good time.*
Amitiés	*Affectionately*
Amicalement	*Yours/Best Wishes/Regards*

À bientôt!

The day for the visitors to return to the U.S. has arrived. It's time to say good-bye.

1re Étape   Au revoir!

On the day of the visitors' departure, say good-bye to the new students you've met during the exchange. Use the phrases in the **Vocabulaire** box and others you've learned in class. Since this is an exchange trip, you'll see each other again soon!

Vocabulaire

Bon voyage!	*Have a good trip!*
sympathique	*nice, likable*
Écris-moi!	*Write!*
revoir	*to see again*

2e Étape   Le courrier

A. After the visitors have returned to the U.S., both groups of students sit down to write notes to their new friends. If you were a visitor, write a thank-you note to your host. If you were one of the hosts, write a note to your guest, giving the date and time of your arrival in the U.S. for the second part of the exchange trip. Use one of the examples on page 23 as a model. The letters to hosts who have chosen a new identity should have their real names on the back so your teacher can distribute the letters.

Connexions

☑ Art

Cher Vincent,

Salut! Comment ça va? Merci beaucoup pour ton hospi-
talité. Tes parents et ta sœur sont très sympathiques.
Ta maison est très belle.

À bientôt!

Chris

Chère Liz,

Bonjour de Québec! Comment vas-tu? J'arrive aux États-
Unis le 12 octobre. Nous arrivons à 16 heures. Je suis
très impatiente de te revoir! À bientôt!

Amitiés,

Béatrice

B. Give your letter to your teacher, who'll deliver it to your exchange partner. Read the letter you've received. If you need help understanding it, consult your teacher.

3ᵉ Étape   L'album

Add the letter you've received to your portfolio. Now you have a complete record of your exchange trip! Decorate the cover of your portfolio and give it a title, such as **Mon voyage à** ___ (*My trip to* ___).

Un calendrier des fêtes francophones

Using your knowledge of holidays, celebrations, and the cultures of French-speaking countries and regions, you will help make a Francophone calendar, working in groups. Your work will be combined with that of other groups to make a yearlong calendar. In the process, you will:

- Research the major legal holidays of one French-speaking country or region and compare them to the U.S. legal holidays
- Determine what special occasions are observed in your chosen French-speaking country or region, including when, why, and how they are celebrated
- Pay special attention to one holiday that is common to all French-speaking countries and regions
- Use the information you've gathered to put together a holiday calendar that you can use throughout the year
- Hold a Francophone celebration

Amusez-vous bien!

Connexions

In the process of making a holiday calendar, you'll sharpen your skills in many areas.

- ✔ Art
- ✔ Géographie
- ✔ Histoire
- ☐ Mathématiques
- ☐ Médias

- ✔ Musique
- ☐ Santé et nutrition
- ☐ Sciences
- ✔ Stratégies d'étude
- ✔ Technologie

Look for the **Connexions** boxes throughout this project.

Warm-up: Les jours fériés aux États-Unis

L ike every country, the U.S. has its legal holidays as well as other special celebrations. At these times, Americans commemorate occasions and traditions important to the entire country or to a particular region. Government offices and many businesses may close, and there may be public or private celebrations. Let's take a look at U.S. holidays, which can give you clues to what's celebrated in French-speaking countries and regions.

Ressources utiles

■ Calendar with U.S. holidays
■ Folder to use for the calendar project

A. Your teacher will divide the class into groups. Each group will make a calendar for a French-speaking country or region. In your group, use a calendar to make a list of U.S. holidays and give their dates.

B. In your group, discuss in English or French the reason for each holiday and decide which of the following categories each holiday belongs to. Some holidays may fit in more than one group.

• Political—related to government

• Military—related to a war, armed victory, or veterans

• Civil—related to an event or an idea that is neither political nor military

• Religious

• Historical

• Other categories

c. When you've finished, report your findings to the class and discuss your ideas together. Put your notes in your calendar folder.

Saviez-vous que...?

The events that a country celebrates and the dates on which they're commemorated can change. France didn't celebrate Bastille Day as its national holiday until 1880, although the event occurred in 1789. The U.S. used to celebrate November 11 as Armistice Day, the day World War I (1914–1918) officially ended. After the Korean War (1950–1953), the name for the November 11 holiday was changed to Veterans' Day in honor of the veterans of all U.S. wars. At present, some states celebrate it and others don't. For some Americans, remembering veterans is now part of the Memorial Day commemoration in May.

Les jours fériés des pays francophones

The French-speaking countries and regions wouldn't celebrate Columbus Day, of course, but do they have legal holidays like Thanksgiving or Independence Day? You're going to find out!

Ressources utiles

■ Books and magazines about international holidays and French-speaking people and cultures

■ Guidebooks for French-speaking countries and regions

■ French-English dictionary

■ Legal Holidays Worksheet 2.Λ.1

■ Holiday Comparison Worksheet 2.A.2

■ The World Wide Web

■ Folder

1ʳᵉ Étape   ## Quels sont les jours fériés des pays francophones?

A. Work with your group to find the major legal holidays of a French-speaking country or region, using some of the resources listed in the **Ressources utiles** box. List each day in French with its English translation on Legal Holidays Worksheet 2.A.1 under **Le jour férié**. As you do your research, record in French or English when and why each holiday is celebrated under **La date** and **La raison**. Be sure to keep a list of the resources for later use.

B. In your group, categorize the holidays, using the same groupings you did for U.S. holidays—**fête politique, militaire, civile, religieuse, historique**. Add any other categories that would apply. While your discussion may be in English, use the French names for the holidays and the categories. Record your results under **Le type de fête** on Legal Holidays Worksheet 2.A.1.

Connexions

☑ Histoire
☑ Technologie

Explorons le Web!

Official agencies of French-speaking countries are a good source of information about holidays in those countries. At the Government, Reference, Travel, or Society and Culture sections of a Web guide, use the keywords to the right to help you in your search about your country.

Keywords

"ambassade (de France, du Sénégal, etc.)"
consulat
name of holiday
fêtes

c. Now present your findings to the class. While your discussion may be in English, use the French names for the holidays. Be sure to put your worksheets in your calendar folder.

2ᵉ Étape Comparez les fêtes!

A. In your group, compare in English how U.S. and Francophone holidays are alike. Be sure to use the French names for the holidays. Do Americans and French speakers celebrate the same kinds of events? In English, record at least two similarities on Holiday Comparison Worksheet 2.A.2.

B. Now search for differences. While the discussion in your group may be in English, use the French names for the holidays. What category do most French-speaking holidays belong to? What about U.S. holidays? Do Americans and French speakers celebrate comparable holidays but at different times of the year? Discuss and record at least two differences in English on Holiday Comparison Worksheet 2.A.2.

c. In English, present the similarities and differences to the class.

Saviez-vous que...?

The French know how to make the best of their vacation time. If a holiday falls on a Tuesday or Thursday, Monday or Friday usually becomes a holiday, too. This is known as **faire le pont** (*to make a bridge*). Unfortunately, if a holiday falls on a Saturday or Sunday, French people don't get Friday or Monday off. Under the law, employees may take legal holidays, but employers have to pay them only for **la Fête du Travail** (May 1). In reality, most people *do* get paid for all legal holidays, because of union contracts.

La chasse aux trésors

Although you may not get the day off from school, you know that many other special days are celebrated throughout the year in the U.S.—Valentine's Day and April Fool's Day, for example. There are also many local holidays, such as Patriots' Day in Massachusetts, or Mardi Gras in New Orleans. What can you find out about such holidays in the French-speaking world?

Ressources utiles

- Books, guidebooks, and magazines on international holidays and French-speaking people and cultures
- French-English dictionary
- Special Days Worksheet 2.B
- The World Wide Web
- Folder

1re Étape   Explorez les fêtes

In your group, research four special days or occasions that are celebrated in your French-speaking country or region. Gather all the information you can on these events. If possible, find pictures of people celebrating these holidays and of things connected with these celebrations. Use the materials listed in the **Ressources utiles** box for help. For each day or occasion, fill in the chart on Special Days Worksheet 2.B.

Vocabulaire

la fête a lieu le [date]	the holiday takes place on [date]
célébrer	to celebrate
commémorer	to commemorate

Connexions

- ☑ Art
- ☑ Géographie
- ☑ Histoire
- ☑ Technologie

Explorons le Web!

How to find holidays will depend greatly on what you've chosen. Most Web guides do not have a section called Holidays, so look under sections labeled Culture, Social, or Society for references. You may also want to refer to the Web sites of consulates and embassies, if you've already found some interesting information there. If you search by holiday name, remember that it's best to use French names. Otherwise you'll be referred to holidays all over the world. Don't forget to bookmark useful Web sites for future reference.

Keywords

fêtes
name of holiday
"wtg-online"

2ᵉ Étape   Partagez vos découvertes

Now with your group, get together with another group in the class and share information. Take turns asking and answering in French, if possible, the following questions about the special celebrations in your countries.

Comment s'appelle la fête? Quand est-ce que cette fête se passe? Quelle est la raison *(reason)* pour cette fête? Comment célèbre-t-on *(How do you celebrate)* cette fête?

3ᵉ Étape   Une affiche pour la fête

Using the information and visuals you gathered in the **1ʳᵉ Étape**, create a poster in French to advertise one of the special **fêtes** of your country. Include the date, name, and other relevant information and symbols. Make it attractive, and hang it on the wall of your classroom for everyone to see.

Saviez-vous que...?

There are several June events that you might look forward to if you lived in France. In Paris, waiters race each other while carrying a glass and a bottle on a tray at **La course des garçons de café**. Movie theater owners select a day in June for **la fête du cinéma**. After you watch one film at the full price, you can see as many other movies as you can cram into the day, each for only one franc! On June 21, all of France goes out to celebrate **la fête de la musique**. Streets and halls are filled with musicians, performers, and free concerts to celebrate the arrival of summer.

Décrivez une fête commune!

It just wouldn't be July 4 without . . . a picnic at the lake? fireworks? a parade? What would you say? Each U.S. holiday has its own festivities. How do French-speaking people celebrate their holidays? Pick a holiday common to all groups and describe it.

Ressources utiles

- Legal Holidays Worksheet 2.A.1
- Special Days Worksheet 2.B
- Books on international holidays
- Books on French-speaking people and cultures
- Guidebooks for French-speaking countries and regions
- French-English dictionary
- Folder

1ʳᵉ Étape **Quelles sont les fêtes communes?**

You know the names, dates, and reasons for your group's holidays. Now you'll discuss what holidays the French-speaking world has in common.

A. As a class, take turns asking each other in French about the holidays celebrated in different Francophone countries. Refer to Worksheets 2.A.1 and 2.B and follow the model below to find out what holidays are common to all the countries or regions studied. Make a list together.

▶ Est-ce que les Suisses fêtent Pâques?
  Oui, les Suisses fêtent Pâques.

▶ Est-ce que les Belges fêtent le 14 juillet?
  Non, les Belges ne fêtent pas le 14 juillet.

Connexions

- ☑ Art
- ☑ Histoire
- ☑ Musique
- ☑ Technologie

B. Select one common holiday that all groups will investigate. First discuss the possible choices. While your discussion may be in English, use the French names for the holidays. Choose a secretary to list the suggested holidays in French on the board. At the end of the discussion, take a vote. Voters for each holiday raise their hands and count off aloud in French. The secretary records the votes and announces the class choice.

> *Secretary:*   Combien votent pour [le jour de l'An]?
> *Voters:*   Un, deux, etc.
>
> *(Repeat for each common holiday.)*
>
> *Secretary:*   Le choix de la classe est [la fête du Travail].

2ᵉ Étape   Comment célèbre-t-on cette fête?

A. Now find out how your group's country celebrates the holiday your class has chosen. In your group, use some of the resources listed in the **Ressources utiles** box to answer the following questions in English. You'll use the answers to prepare a brief report to the class.

1. How is the holiday celebrated? Are there private events with friends and relatives at home? Are there any public events, such as parades, fireworks, and dances?

2. Are any special foods served? Describe them.

3. Are there any special clothes or colors that people wear? What do the clothes or colors represent?

4. What special music or songs are played? Why? Provide examples, if you can.

5. What special places, symbols, or flowers do people associate with this day? Why? Provide examples, if you can.

Un @ peu plus

Write a brief paragraph in French explaining how your group's country celebrates the holiday your class has chosen. The holiday vocabulary in the Almanac will help you.

B. With your group, prepare a short oral and visual presentation in English or French about how your country celebrates this holiday and present it to the class. If your presentation is in French and you have a paragraph in French, include it here (see the **Un peu plus** activity on page 33). Include any pictures, drawings, and music you found.

C. After each group has given its presentation, have a class discussion about the similarities and differences in the celebrations.

Saviez-vous que...?

In France, April Fool's Day is called **Poisson d'avril**, since traditionally children try to stick pictures of fish (**les poissons**) on the backs of their friends. The tradition of treating April 1 as a day for practical jokes dates back to the switch from the Julian calendar (created by Julius Caesar) to the Gregorian calendar (created by Pope Gregory XIII and generally adopted by the eighteenth century). Under the new calendar, April 1 was no longer the first day of the new year, so New Year's gifts or good wishes became a bit of a joke on that day.

Votre beau calendrier

N ow that you have the information you need, it's time to decide on the final details and assemble the Francophone calendar.

Ressources utiles

■ The materials in your calendar folder

■ Tagboard or large pieces of butcher paper

■ Art supplies, such as markers, rulers, etc.

■ A 12-month calendar covering the current school year

1re Étape — Quel symbole représente chaque fête?

Using your worksheets and the materials and notes in your folder, consider what you now know about each of the holidays in your French-speaking country or region—its purpose, the way it's celebrated, and the common colors and symbols that people use for it. With your group, decide how you want to represent each holiday on the calendar. You might draw something or use pictures that you found in your research.

2e Étape — Le partage des tâches

You need to make some basic decisions on the actual making of the calendar. How will you divide the tasks?

A. In class, decide how you want to divide the work. Do you want each group to work on one part of the year, creating the grids and representing the holidays for these months? Or do you want each group to have a particular task? Make these decisions with the help of your teacher.

Connexions

 Art
☑ Histoire
☑ Technologie

B. Next, decide with the class how you want to set up the calendar pages. Be creative. Use the questions below to guide you.

- Where will the name of the month be? across the top? down the side? along the bottom?

- Will all the grids be the same color? different colors?

- Where will the names of the countries or regions be listed? on the cover page?

- What art do you want to include to represent each month?

Remember that **lundi** is generally the first day of the week on a French calendar!

Saviez-vous que ...?

In France and in most of the Catholic French-speaking countries and regions, people celebrate their name days. Each day of the year marks the feast of a particular saint or an important event in the Catholic Church. Saints' days are included on most French calendars, and daily newspapers and weather reports will give the day's saint and sometimes briefly tell the story of the saint. To mark the occasion, children named after that saint receive cards, candies, or small gifts. To wish someone a happy name day, simply say: **Bonne fête!**

Explorons le Web

Can you find your name day? If you don't find your first name, try your middle name. Having a name day is like having two birthdays a year!

Keywords

"Catholic calendar"
"Catholic Online Saints"

3ᵉ Étape — Décorez et assemblez les pages du calendrier

A. In your group, divide up the tasks of making the calendar pages, and get to work! Make sure you have all the information you need from the other groups.

B. Assemble your work as a class, making sure everything is in place. After your calendar is created, if you wish, add the name days and birthdays of your group members to your calendar.

C. Display the calendar and admire your handiwork. You've made a resource that you can use all year!

Vocabulaire

La fête se passe ___	*The holiday takes place ___*
aimer mieux	*to prefer*
J'aime mieux	*I prefer*
l'événement *(m.)*	*event, happening*
favori/favorite	*favorite*

4ᵉ Étape   ## Quelle est la fête favorite de la classe?

Think about all the different **fêtes** that your class has discussed and decide which one is your favorite. In your group, take turns asking and answering questions, following the model below. When everyone has finished, determine the favorite **fête** of your group. Then take a class vote to determine the favorite **fête** of the class. If that celebration appears on your group's calendar, mark it in a special way.

▶ —[*Classmate's name*], quelle est ta fête favorite?
—Moi, je préfère [la fête des Rois]. Et toi?
—Ma fête favorite est [le 14 juillet].

Célébrons!

After all the hard work you've done, you deserve to celebrate! Celebrate holidays the way French-speaking people do. Think colors, sounds, and excitement everywhere.

1re Étape   Quelles fêtes voulez-vous célébrer?

As a class, decide how you want to celebrate and organize the party. Do you want to celebrate the class's favorite holiday (see Section D, **4e Étape**)? Do you want to celebrate the holiday coming up next on the calendar? Or do you want to celebrate a mix of the Francophone holidays you studied? Discuss the options with your teacher.

2e Étape   L'organisation

You should now decide on the logistics of this celebration. What do you want to prepare for the celebration? Will you have guests coming to the party? How will you invite them? Where will you hold the party? Will there be food? How will you divide the work? Make sure you use your worksheets and the materials in your folders to help you present the holidays. You might want to choose a volunteer or two to prepare a checklist of what's needed and to supervise the preparation.

3e Étape   Amusez-vous!

Has everything been taken care of? You are now ready to celebrate and answer questions about the Francophone holidays. Enjoy!

Saviez-vous que...?

French Polynesians know how to celebrate. In July they hold the month-long **Heiva i Tahiti** festival, which features the prestigious Miss Heiva i Tahiti Beauty Contest. It also features music, dancing, dancing competitions, and an arts and crafts display. The highlight of this festival is French Bastille Day on July 14. These festivities are to Tahiti what Carnival is to Brazil, and people come from all over to be part of it.

La chambre idéale

In this project, you and your group will design your dream bedroom! At the end of the project, your class will award prizes to the best rooms in several categories. As part of this project, you will:

- Choose categories and make prizes for the room competition
- Design the style, color, and décor of your room
- Select appropriate furniture
- Prepare an exhibit and make a presentation of your room
- Hold a design festival and award the prizes

Soyez créatifs!

Connexions

As you design your room, you'll sharpen your skills in many areas.

- ✔ Art
- ☐ Géographie
- ✔ Histoire
- ☐ Mathématiques
- ☐ Médias
- ☐ Musique
- ☐ Santé et nutrition
- ☐ Sciences
- ✔ Stratégies d'étude
- ✔ Technologie

Look for the **Connexions** boxes throughout this project.

Warm-up: Les goûts et les couleurs

A. Work with the same group of three or four of your classmates for this entire project. Each group member should bring in at least two photos or drawings of student rooms or bedrooms from magazines, catalogs, books, and so on. In French, describe each of your rooms to your group. Then as a group, write a list of features that you like and dislike in the rooms.

▶ La couleur noire nous plaît.
Les chaises ne nous plaisent pas.
Ce petit lit nous plaît beaucoup.

B. Now, interview some other members of your class in French to find out which features appeal to them and which don't.

▶ [Matt], aimez-vous les vieilles lampes?
Oui, je les aime.
Non, je ne les aime pas.

C. In your group, share the information that you've gathered and add it to your list of likes and dislikes.

▶ [Matt] aime les vieilles lampes.
[Jennifer] n'aime pas les vieilles lampes.

D. Review your list of likes and dislikes. Are there any features that were liked or disliked by more than one student? Circle them on your list and keep the list for reference when designing your room.

Saviez-vous que ...?

The most important characteristics of current French home decorating are comfort and the desire to reflect one's own personality. Almost half the French express a preference for the simple wooden furniture traditionally typical of rural areas, just as many Americans like colonial furniture. Another quarter prefer antiques, but most actually use reproductions rather than the real thing. Younger people tend to prefer modern furniture. In reality, present-day homes are often decorated in a mixture of styles, including those borrowed from other cultures, especially Asia and South America. Another trend in French decorating parallels what has happened in the U.S. More and more money is being spent on items associated with how people spend their free time—color televisions, large-screen televisions, VCRs, stereo systems, and so forth.

Le concours

At the design festival, prizes will be given for the best rooms in several categories. Create these categories now so that you'll have a goal in mind as you complete the design of your ideal room.

Ressources utiles

▨ Ballot Worksheet 3.A
▨ Cardboard or sturdy paper
▨ Scissors, tape, glue
▨ Computer and word-processing program
▨ Folder for storing worksheets and creative ideas

1ʳᵉ Étape   Les différentes catégories

A. Working in your small group, brainstorm in French three possible prize categories to be used in your room competition. Be creative!

▶ Une chambre très amusante
Une chambre avec des couleurs éclatantes
Une chambre très originale
Une chambre très moderne

B. For each category, write a short description in English of the criteria that will be used when choosing a winner in that category.

▶ **Une chambre avec des couleurs éclatantes:** This room must contain at least three prominent colors in its décor and be bright and cheerful.

Connexions

☑ Art
☑ Stratégies
   d'étude

2ᵉ Étape   Le vote

Share your ideas for categories with your class. Vote as a class and choose four to eight categories to be used in the competition. Copy the categories the class chooses onto Ballot Worksheet 3.A. You'll use this ballot when it's time to vote.

3ᵉ Étape   Préparez les prix

A. Divide the chosen categories with their descriptions among the groups in your class. Each group will make prizes to award to the winner of its categories. You may choose to make ribbons, medals, certificates, or trophies. Use the materials in the **Ressources utiles** box to help you.

B. Put the prizes, the descriptions of the categories, and Ballot Worksheet 3.A away until the day of the competition. File the categories and descriptions in your folder.

Saviez-vous que ...?

About 55 percent of the French own homes, and they are the ones most satisfied with their housing. Why? In general, there's more space per person than in apartments. The vast majority of homeowners have garages but only a little more than a third of apartment dwellers do. Home ownership offers another great benefit for the French, who in general love to garden. More than 90 percent of homes have enough land for a garden, and in one out of three of those homes, there are indeed gardens.

Les décisions fondamentales

Now it's time to begin designing your ideal bedroom. You'll need to make some general decisions first. This is your chance to be creative!

Ressources utiles

- Cardboard or sturdy paper
- Style Worksheet 3.B
- Magazines showing decorating ideas
- Art books or pictures of artwork from the French-speaking world
- Encyclopedias

1re Étape   Le style

Working with your group, you'll need to decide on the décor of your room. Do you want it to be traditional? futuristic? Should it have a theme, such as a particular movie, time period, or sport?

 A. When you've chosen a style, write a description of it in English on Style Worksheet 3.B.

 B. Now consider how you will achieve this look. Will it be with wallpaper? a mural? furniture? On Style Worksheet 3.B, write a general description of ways that your style can be established in your room. When you're finished, put it in your folder. You'll make final decisions later. Make sure you choose specific competition categories.

Connexions
- ✔ Art
- ✔ Histoire

Un peu plus

Choose an influence from the French-speaking world to include in your room's décor, such as the bright, bold colors and designs from French Polynesia, or a design showing the Muslim influence in North Africa. Record your ideas on Style Worksheet 3.B with the description of your room. Use the materials in the **Ressources utiles** box to help you.

2ᵉ Étape   Les couleurs

Now decide which colors will work best with this style. Maybe metallic colors would look great in your space-age room. Or perhaps you'd like bright blues to complement a nautical theme. Refer to the Almanac for a list of colors. Choose colors for the walls (**les murs**), floor (**le plancher**) or floor covering, and even ceiling (**le plafond**). Record your choices in French on Style Worksheet 3.B.

3ᵉ Étape   Les détails de la décoration

Finally, decide what kinds of floor, window, and wall coverings you'll use in your room. Use the words for furniture and furnishings in the Almanac to help you. Record your choices in French on Style Worksheet 3.B, and place it in your folder.

C Le mobilier

Your ideal room wouldn't be complete without plenty of interesting furniture. Keeping in mind the style of your room, design your furnishings!

Ressources utiles

- Decorating magazines, mail-order catalogs
- Catalogs from furniture and department stores
- Original drawings/descriptions of creative décor
- The World Wide Web

1re Étape Combien de meubles et quels meubles?

In your group, make general decisions about the furniture you'll want to have in your room. Make a list in French of the items and the quantities. Refer to the list of furniture and furnishings in the Almanac as needed.

▶ 1 lit
2 fauteuils
1 table

2e Étape Plusieurs possibilités

As homework or in class, look through decorating magazines, store and mail-order catalogs, and the Web to find some of the pieces of furniture on your list. Draw or cut out several options for each item on your list, so that your group has possibilities to choose from.

Connexions

- ☑ Art
- ☑ Technologie

Explorons le Web!

Many furniture and furnishings stores and companies advertise on the Web. Their ads often include pictures of their products. To locate such Web sites, try using a search engine that has versions for French-speaking countries or regions. For example, if you are using Yahoo!, click on France at the bottom of the page and then follow one of these paths: **meubles, maison et jardin, achats en ligne,** or **acheter, acheter-moins-cher.** Scan the brief descriptions of the selected Web sites and investigate the ones that look promising.

3e Étape   Le mobilier idéal

Finally, in your group, choose the furniture items that you feel best complement your room's style. Refer to your list of furniture to make sure that you choose enough items. Save your pictures and drawings of furniture to prepare your room for the competition.

Saviez-vous que ...?

In French decorating, pastel colors are fashionable but bright colors are becoming more popular. Also **en vogue** (*in fashion*) is furniture made from wicker and from wood combined with glass or iron. Instead of large pieces, the French are changing to furniture that helps save space and can be used in different places or in various ways. These pieces include folding chairs; stacking tables; modular pieces for desks, bookcases, computers, and stereo systems; hide-a-beds; and so forth. So consider these characteristics when you're decorating your bedroom.

Montez l'exposition

Now decide how you're going to present your room visually during the design festival. Do you want to make a drawing of your room design and label the features in French? Or draw it using a computer drawing program? Do you think a poster with cut-out pictures will work best? Would you like to make a three-dimensional model of the room, such as a diorama? The possibilities are numerous!

Ressources utiles

- Cardboard boxes
- Scissors, tape, glue, markers, paints
- Computer with drawing software
- Pictures or drawings of furniture

1re Étape — Comment allez-vous montrer votre chambre?

Discover your group's talents and decide how to present your room to your class during the competition. If you're artistic, consider using those talents to make a painting, drawing, or model of your room. If you enjoy working with computers, try out a drawing or paint program. Find a style of presentation that uses everyone's talents.

2e Étape — La création

Once your group has decided on how to present your room, it's time to get to work! Remember to include in some way all of the decisions that you made earlier on colors, style, and furnishings. Put them all together into a finished visual product, ready for the design festival.

Connexions

 Art
 Stratégies d'étude
 Technologie

3ᵉ Étape **Préparez votre présentation**

Finally, create short descriptive labels in French for your display. Label the furniture and furnishings, give your room a title, and highlight four or five features that make your room special. Prepare what each group member will say in French for your presentation.

Un peu plus

Write a composition or poem in French describing the unique features of your ideal room. You may mount it, and then illustrate it.

Que le concours commence!

The day of the design festival has arrived! Your room and those of your competitors will be on display. Today you will be both competitor and judge of the competition!

Ressources utiles

░ Prizes and descriptions of categories

░ Ballot Worksheet 3.A

░ Your room presentation

1re Étape   Passez en revue les catégories

Before starting the competition, review the categories that you recorded on Ballot Worksheet 3.A by which the rooms will be judged. Each group will briefly read to the class the names and descriptions of its competition categories.

2e Étape   Exposez vos créations

Now it's time for the competition to begin! Display your room presentation and have each member of your group describe a few important features of your room to the class. After each group has given its presentation, take turns answering questions about your display and visiting the other displays. Be prepared to ask questions and make comments in French while you visit. Take notes on Ballot Worksheet 3.A as you view each presentation.

Connexions

 Art

3ᵉ Étape Le vote final

It's time to vote for the winner in each category. Each class member votes on each category and gives the completed Ballot Worksheet 3.A to the teacher, who will tally the results.

4ᵉ Étape La remise des prix

After the vote, the teacher awards a prize to the winning presentation for each category. Celebrate your victories! Display your group's presentation in the classroom.

Vocabulaire

Félicitations!	*Congratulations!*
le gagnant/la gagnante	*the winner*
Les gagnants du prix pour [une chambre très originale] sont ___.	*The winners of the prize for [a very creative room] are ___.*

Et si on jouait?

U sing your knowledge of games and Francophone cultures, you and your group will make a board game. In the process, you will:

- Make up questions and answers in French about daily life
- Research one or more French-speaking countries or areas and make up questions and answers in English
- Write directions for the game
- Design and make a game board
- Test the game board and rules
- Share your game with your classmates

À vous de jouer!

Connexions

In the process of making a game, and depending on what topics you choose for your game, you'll sharpen your skills in many areas, including these:

- ✔ Art
- ✔ Géographie
- ☐ Histoire
- ☐ Mathématiques
- ☐ Médias

- ☐ Musique
- ☐ Santé et nutrition
- ☐ Sciences
- ✔ Stratégies d'étude
- ✔ Technologie

Look for the **Connexions** boxes throughout this project.

Warm-up: **Parlons de vos jeux préférés**

Y ou probably have a few favorite games. Why are they your favorites? Some people like short and simple games, while others prefer games that involve more complex strategy. Still others like the excitement of games in which luck is an important ingredient. Perhaps you prefer the physical dexterity and quick thinking that are part of video games. Find out what games you and your fellow group members like to play and why.

A. Form a small group of four to six students. Name your favorite games in English and explain why you like them. Read the **Saviez-vous que ... ?** box to find out the French names of some popular games.

B. In your group, brainstorm any French words and expressions you know that have to do with games.

C. In your group, talk in French about the types of games you prefer to play: for example, board, card, or computer games. The **Vocabulaire** box and the illustrations that follow will help you.

Saviez-vous que ...?

M any popular French board games are probably familiar to you: **les dames** (*checkers*), **le jeu de loto** (a game similar to bingo), **les échecs** (*chess*), **les dominos, le Monopoly, le Scrabble,** and **le Trivial Pursuit.** French board games for children often resemble American children's games but have different names. **Le jeu de l'oie** (*The Goose's Game*) is for younger children. Players throw dice and move the number of squares shown on the dice. The first player to reach the goose wins the game. In **Les petits chevaux** (*The Little Horses*), players try to get their horses out of the stable, around the board, and up to the finish line first.

Vocabulaire

jouer à	*to play (a game or sport)*
À quels jeux est-ce que tu aimes jouer?	*What kinds of games do you like to play?*
J'aime jouer au Trivial Pursuit.	*I like to play Trivial Pursuit.*
Je préfère jouer aux échecs.	*I prefer to play chess.*

jouer aux échecs

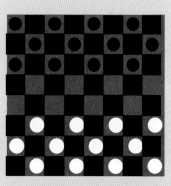

jouer aux dames

les jeux de société

jouer aux jeux électroniques

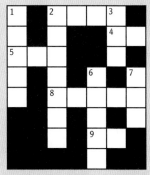

faire des mots croisés

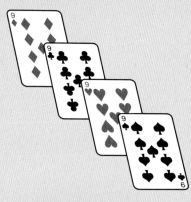

jouer aux cartes

Des questions pour jouer

Y ou've been asking and answering questions in French ever since you started studying the language. You may not realize it, but you can make a board game using those questions and answers—and that's what you're going to do!

Ressources utiles

- 3" x 5" cards in one color
- Question Worksheet 4.A
- Folder or binder to compile Worksheets and other materials

1ʳᵉ Étape   ### Qu'est-ce que vous savez?

A. What kinds of questions can you ask in your game? Start with everything you've learned to say in French so far. Build on simple questions by adding a phrase, such as **à ta droite** (*on your right*) or **à ta gauche** (*on your left*) or ask about someone's family members.

▶ Comment t'appelles-tu?
Comment s'appelle cette jeune fille?
Comment s'appelle la jeune fille à ta droite?
Comment s'appelle ta sœur?

How many variations of these questions can you come up with? Brainstorm and record a list with your group.

B. In your group, read through the topics under **Sujets** on Question Worksheet 4.A. Check off topics that you know how to ask questions about. If you can think of any other topics, write them under **Autres sujets**.

Connexions

☑ Stratégies d'étude

2ᵉ Étape   Écrivez des questions et des réponses

Form pairs within your group, and divide the topics among the pairs. Work with your partner to write 5–10 questions and answers in French for each of your topics. Record them on Question Worksheet 4.A. Use the back of the worksheet if necessary. Some questions will have only one possible answer (**De quelle couleur est la neige?**), while others will have answers that vary (**Où habites-tu?**).

▶ *Question:*   Où habites-tu?
   Possible response: J'habite [15], rue [boulevard] Cypress.

   Question: Quel âge a ton frère?
   Possible response: Il a ___ ans.

   Question: Combien de frères et de sœurs as-tu?
   Possible responses: J'ai ___ frère(s) et ___ sœur(s).
                         Je n'ai pas de frères.
                         Je n'ai qu'une sœur.

   Question: Quel est ton numéro de téléphone?
   Possible response: Mon numéro de téléphone est ___.

Saviez-vous que ...?

In the U.S., one phone number is used throughout the country for police, fire, and medical emergency services (911). In France, there are different numbers for each emergency service. The number for the police (**la police**) is 17. It is 18 for firefighters (**les pompiers**), and 15 or 18 for emergency medical assistance (**SAMU—Service d'aide médicale d'urgence**).

3ᵉ Étape   Sélectionnez les questions et les réponses

A. Trade questions with another pair in your group and check each other's French. If you disagree or are unsure about what's correct, see if you can come to an agreement as a group before consulting with your teacher. Work together to make the best possible questions and answers.

B. Get back together with your group and look at the questions and answers that each pair has written. If possible, come up with additional questions and answers. Delete any duplicate questions.

C. Finally, write all the questions and answers on 3" x 5" cards of the same color. Use a separate card for each question and answer. Write the question on one side and its answer on the other.

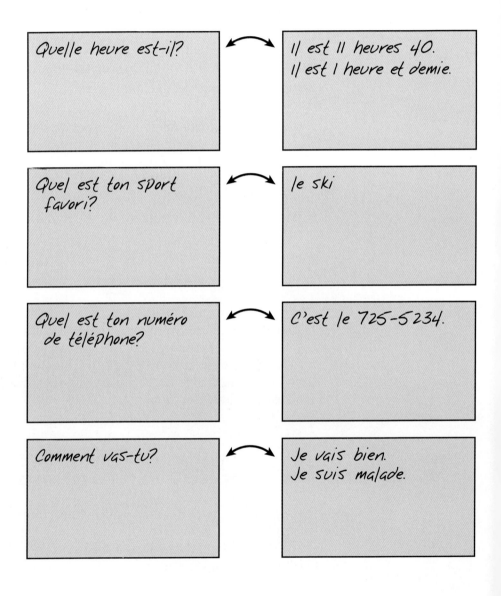

Quelle heure est-il? ↔ Il est 11 heures 40. / Il est 1 heure et demie.

Quel est ton sport favori? ↔ le ski

Quel est ton numéro de téléphone? ↔ C'est le 725-5234.

Comment vas-tu? ↔ Je vais bien. / Je suis malade.

Les questions culturelles

Keep your game interesting and exciting by preparing questions in English about one or more French-speaking countries or regions.

Ressources utiles

■ World map and Francophone maps

■ Books and magazines about Francophone history and culture

■ Encyclopedias and almanacs

■ Travel magazines and brochures about the Francophone world

■ 3" x 5" cards in a color different from those in Section A

■ Folder

■ The World Wide Web

1re Étape

Quelles sortes de questions culturelles?

A. In your group, discuss what subjects relating to the Francophone world seem interesting to you. There are French-speaking countries and regions on every continent. You may know very little about some of them, so you might want to do a little research before choosing your topics. Below and on the next page are a few sample topics:

- The geography, history, and/or famous people of a French-speaking country or region

- Daily life in a French-speaking country or region: family, food, school, and pastimes

- Popular French-speaking musicians and actors; film or music festivals

Connexions

☑ Géographie
☑ Stratégies d'étude
☑ Technologie

- Sporting events: car races (Paris–Dakar, Le Mans), bicycle races (the **Tour de France**), tennis tournaments (the French Open), World Cup soccer

- Vacationing in the Caribbean

- Capital cities of French-speaking countries

B. As a class, decide if all the groups will make games based on the same topics, different topics, or a mixture of the two. Then, in groups or as a class, select topics. Decide whether one topic or many would work best with your game and whether you want to have a special challenge section or some bonus questions. Remember that the cultural questions and answers you prepare on the French-speaking world will be in English.

Trouvez des renseignements intéressants!

Form pairs within your group and divide the research work according to your group's preferences. Using the sources listed in the **Ressources utiles** box on page 61, make up a list of 5–10 possible questions for each topic. Include pictures of famous places and things if you wish. Be sure to keep notes about the sources you use, since you may have to go back later to find more information.

Un peu plus

Make your game more challenging by creating some additional questions in French. Base your questions on expressions you already know.

▶ *You already know*	*Variation*
Quel/Quelle est ___?	Quelle est la capitale de la Belgique?
Quelle est la date de ___?	Quelle est la date de la fête nationale de la France?
Qui est/Comment s'appelle ___?	Qui est/Comment s'appelle le premier ministre de la France?
De quelle couleur ___?	De quelle couleur est le drapeau québécois?

3ᵉ Étape — Choisissez les questions

A. When you and your partner have finished your list, trade questions and answers with another pair. Check each other's lists to make the best possible questions and most accurate answers. In your small group, read all the questions and answers and delete any duplicates.

B. Write your cultural questions and answers in English on 3" x 5" cards. Be sure to use cards of a different color from those used in Section A. Write the question on one side of the card and the answer on the other. If you wrote any cultural questions in French (for the **Un peu plus** activity on page 62), file that list in your folder for the moment.

Saviez-vous que ...?

French speakers like card games. One popular children's game, **le jeu des sept familles,** is similar to Old Maid. Players ask each other for cards. The goal is to get all the members in a family—children, parents, and grandparents—so you can lay down your cards. **Mille bornes,** a game about a car trip, is for older children and adults. **Mille bornes** is also available in the U.S. **Le bridge** and **la belote** are popular card games with adults. Unlike bridge, **la belote** uses cards from 7 through the ace (**l'as**). Different combinations of cards are worth different points.

Les règles du jeu

L ike all games, your board game needs a set of rules. Look at other games to help you decide what the objective, the rules, and the organization of your own game will be.

Ressources utiles

- World map and Francophone maps
- Several board games and their directions, particularly games that use information or questions on cards
- Rules Worksheet 4.C (2 per group)
- 3" x 5" cards in a third color
- Guidebooks for the French-speaking world
- Folder

1ʳᵉ Étape **Examinez les règles d'un jeu de société**

In your group, choose a particular game and spread out the board and playing pieces. Next, analyze the directions of that game by answering the questions on Rules Worksheet 4.C. Then discuss as a class what the rules of a game include and the order in which they should be explained.

2ᵉ Étape **Quelques décisions préliminaires**

What will be the goal of your game? How will you use your question cards? Make some decisions about the basic procedures and moves of your game. As a group, answer the questions under Basic Decisions on a second copy of Rules Worksheet 4.C, but this time apply them to your game.

Connexions

☑ Stratégies d'étude

Un @ peu plus

Decide what to do with the cultural questions in French that you created in the **Un peu plus** activity in Section B. Will they become a separate set of questions or will you combine them with one of the other sets? Write each one on a 3" x 5" card, the question on one side and the answer on the other. If you are using them in a different way from the other sets of cards, use a third color of cards; otherwise write them on cards of the same color as the set to which they belong.

3ᵉ Étape **Préparez les règles du jeu**

Work with your group to develop some rules for your game. Study the questions under Rules of the Game on Rules Worksheet 4.C to help you make decisions. Write answers applicable to your game on your second copy of the worksheet. You'll probably want to revise some of your rules later as you perfect your game.

4ᵉ Étape **Lisez vos instructions**

In your group, check your directions against what you wrote on Worksheet 4.C. For example, should you add anything to what the players need to play the game? Have you changed your ideas about how to use the question cards? Record any additions or changes. Then write a first draft of your rules. Remember to be very careful about details.

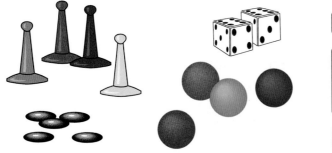  

Saviez-vous que ...?

Les jeux audiovisuels (*computer games*) have become increasingly popular in France as more and more homes have computers. As in the U.S., these games are usually available on CD-ROMs, but in France, interactive games are also available on the **Minitel**. Started in 1983, the **Minitel** was the first system of its kind in the world. The original idea behind the **Minitel** was to put free computer terminals into French homes so that people could purchase goods and services on-line. Subscribers pay only for the time they actually use on the system. The **Minitel** has increased the services it offers, including providing interactive games.

D Le tableau de jeu

The game is starting to come together. Now that you have an idea of what the rules are going to be, you need to design the game board. It has to work with the rules you've written, or else you'll have to change some of the rules.

Ressources utiles

- Several board games and their directions, particularly ones that use information or questions on cards as part of playing the game
- Analyzing a Game Board Worksheet 4.D.1
- First draft of rules for your game
- Our Game Board Worksheet 4.D.2
- Materials for creating the game board: colored markers, cardboard, file folders, poster board, tape
- Folder

1re Étape — Examinez le tableau d'un jeu de société

In Section C, you chose a board game and analyzed its directions. Now analyze the design of the same game's board. Spread out the board and playing pieces. Examine how the game board and the rules work together and identify features that had to be included on the game board because of its rules. For help, answer the questions under Features on Analyzing a Game Board Worksheet 4.D.1. Then complete the rest of the worksheet.

Connexions

- ☑ Art
- ☑ Stratégies d'étude

2ᵉ Étape   Les éléments nécessaires à votre jeu de société

Since you've practiced looking for the features a game board might need, you're better prepared to design your own board. Keep Analyzing a Game Board Worksheet 4.D.1 nearby for reference. With your group, read through the basic game rules again. Look for features that *must* be included on your game board, such as directions that tell players:

* The starting place and the goal
* To go back or forward a number of spaces
* To take an extra turn or to skip a turn
* To choose a particular kind of card
* To go to a particular place on the board
* Where to put particular materials on the board

Record your decisions under Features on Our Game Board Worksheet 4.D.2.

3ᵉ Étape   Le nom du jeu

The name of a game often relates to its goal or to how it's played. In your group, brainstorm some ideas for a French name (you may have to do this in English). Record the suggestions, then take a vote. Record the group's choice under The Name of the Game on Worksheet 4.D.2.

4ᵉ Étape   La décoration du tableau de jeu

A. Keeping in mind the features you *must* have on the game board, discuss with your group how you want the board to look. There are some examples of game boards on the opposite page. Maybe you can adapt one of them to fit your game or come up with something unique. Jot down your decisions under Design on Our Game Board Worksheet 4.D.2 and draw a sketch if you'd like. Decide where to position the name of the game on the board and record that information too.

B. Now brainstorm ideas about how to illustrate some of the topics covered in your board game. What other kinds of decorations do you want to include? Write your decisions under Decorations on Our Game Board Worksheet 4.D.2. As you decide how to illustrate the game board, think about where you might find pictures that you can photocopy, cut and paste, or draw.

5ᵉ Étape   Une première esquisse

Make a first sketch of the game board in the same size as the final board. Be sure to draw in all the shapes and use the actual colors. If there are labels or directions on the board, write some samples to see if there is enough space. Check the sports and games vocabulary in the Almanac for the French expressions you need. As a group, decide who will actually do the sketch. Will one person or a pair of students take full responsibility, or will each group member prepare a different part? Then make the sketch.

Mettez les dernières touches

 efore you can create the final rules and make your game board, you need to do a test run. How well will your rules and game board work together?

Ressources utiles

■ Materials for playing pieces: stones, beans, marbles, dice, wooden/plastic pieces in various shapes

■ Art materials, such as colored markers and glue

■ Materials for the game board itself: cardboard, file folders, poster board, tape

■ Container for the game: box or large envelope with a clasp

■ Folder

1re Étape   ## Essayez le jeu

Use your rough draft of the rules and a sketch of the game board to try out the game. Choose one group member to record any needed changes to the rules or the board while the others play the game in order to find out what works and what doesn't.

2e Étape   ## Perfectionnez votre jeu

In your group, make any necessary changes to the directions or the game board, then play the game again. This time players speak French during the game. Many of the needed expressions are in the sports and games section of the Almanac. Your group may choose to have non-playing members help players use French expressions, so that they can

Connexions

☑ Art
☑ Stratégies
   d'étude

play the game at a reasonable speed. Once again, have one group member record any problems, including additional French expressions that players will need to play the game. You don't need to think of everything that players might say, just expressions that they will have to use often.

3ᵉ Étape   Demandez à un autre groupe d'essayer votre jeu

If students who know nothing about your game can play it by reading the rules, it really works! Ask another group to play your game while a couple of students from your group look on. Your group members can help the other students play your game and record any problems. If there are difficulties, make the needed revisions.

4ᵉ Étape   La boîte pour le jeu

Since you're making this game for yourselves and others to enjoy, it would be a good idea to keep it in some kind of sturdy container. You might consider one file folder for the game board, another for the rules; and plastic bags, a large mailing envelope with a clasp, or a box as a container for the game pieces.

5ᵉ Étape   Le moment est arrivé! Assemblez le jeu!

You're finally ready to put the game together. In your group, divide up the final tasks. Write a final description of the rules (make sure these are easy to read). Do you need additional French expressions for playing the game? If so, make a list. Draw the final game board on the cardboard or poster board provided. Gather any materials necessary for playing the game. Prepare the containers that will hold the game and put in everything you've made and collected for the game. You've worked hard and your game is now ready to share with other groups. Take your show on the road!

Organisez vos jeux Olympiques

Using your knowledge of sports and French-speaking countries and regions, you and your classmates will organize your own mini-Olympics for French-speaking countries and regions. In the process, you will:

- Decide which games to hold (Summer or Winter Olympics)
- Create and compete in 2–6 competitive events
- Prepare the opening ceremonies
- Design costumes or symbol cards and medals, and hold an awards ceremony
- Locate anthems and folk songs of the French-speaking world
- Hold your Olympic Games

You and your classmates will be grouped in committees and will work on many tasks at the same time to prepare for your mini-Olympics.

Que les jeux commencent!

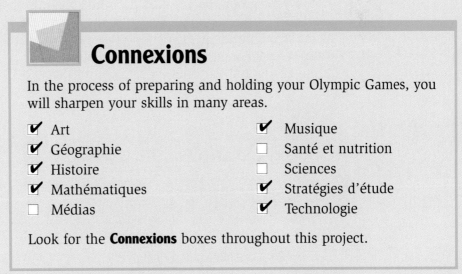

Connexions

In the process of preparing and holding your Olympic Games, you will sharpen your skills in many areas.

- ☑ Art
- ☑ Géographie
- ☑ Histoire
- ☑ Mathématiques
- ☐ Médias
- ☑ Musique
- ☐ Santé et nutrition
- ☐ Sciences
- ☑ Stratégies d'étude
- ☑ Technologie

Look for the **Connexions** boxes throughout this project.

Warm-up: Qu'est-ce que vous savez des jeux Olympiques?

Ressources utiles

■ Olympic Sports Worksheet 5.W

■ French-English dictionary

■ Books about the Olympic Games

■ Portfolio (a three-ring binder with pockets, file jacket, file folder) for each student

■ The World Wide Web

 A. Working with a small group, brainstorm in French a list of sports and write them under Part 1 on Olympic Sports Worksheet 5.W. Write each sport under the season in which it is played. Some sports may be played in more than one season.

 B. In your group, decide which of the sports on your list are Olympic sports. Put a question mark next to any sport that you are uncertain about. Then decide if each sport is part of the Summer Games (**les jeux d'été**) or the Winter Games (**les jeux d'hiver**) and list it under the appropriate heading in Part 2 of the same worksheet.

Saviez-vous que ...?

The first recorded Olympics, held near the town of Olympia in Greece in 77 B.C., consisted of one foot race. The Olympic Games as we know them today began in Athens, Greece, in 1896 through the hard work of the French educator Baron Pierre de Coubertin. He felt that better international understanding could be achieved if young athletes from many countries participated in a series of sporting events.

C. Now work with your group to expand your list of Olympic sports. Use some of the materials listed in the **Ressources utiles** box to find out what sports are played at either the Summer or the Winter Games. (Your teacher will tell your group which games it should investigate.) List at least five sports in French on your Olympic Sports Worksheet 5.W.

 D. Finally, exchange information with the rest of the class and add the new information to Olympic Sports Worksheet 5.W. Put your worksheet in your portfolio.

Explorons le Web!

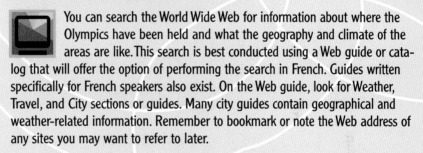 You can search the World Wide Web for information about where the Olympics have been held and what the geography and climate of the areas are like. This search is best conducted using a Web guide or catalog that will offer the option of performing the search in French. Guides written specifically for French speakers also exist. On the Web guide, look for Weather, Travel, and City sections or guides. Many city guides contain geographical and weather-related information. Remember to bookmark or note the Web address of any sites you may want to refer to later.

Jeux d'été ou d'hiver?

ities and regions around the world compete for the privilege of hosting the Olympic Games. In choosing a location for the games, one of the most basic considerations of the International Olympic Committee is the geography of a region. For example, are the mountains suitable for Winter Olympic skiing events and do they receive sufficient snowfall? Are there appropriate bodies of water for Summer Olympic rowing and yachting events? You'll begin to organize your games by deciding which games you'll hold—**les jeux d'été** or **les jeux d'hiver**.

Ressources utiles

- ■ World atlas
- ■ Guidebooks for French-speaking countries
- ■ Books about the Olympic Games
- ■ Which Games? Worksheet 5.A.1
- ■ Committees Worksheet 5.A.2
- ■ Portfolio

1re Étape   ## Le climat et la géographie

Working with your group, brainstorm in French the kinds of climate and geography you think are needed to hold the Olympic Games. Continue with the same games—**les jeux d'été** or **les jeux d'hiver**—that your group discussed in the Warm-up. Each of you should record the group's answers in Part 1 on Which Games? Worksheet 5.A.1. Share your information with the class.

Connexions

☑ Géographie

2ᵉ Étape — Où se sont déroulés les jeux?

A. With your group, find out which French-speaking cities have hosted the Olympics in the past using materials in the **Ressources utiles** box. Record the places in Part 2 of Worksheet 5.A.1 under **Où**. List the games held in each location (**les jeux d'été** or **les jeux d'hiver**) and the year.

B. As a group, choose one of the locations you listed. Find it on a map, and then investigate and record its climate and geography. In Part 3 on the same worksheet, make a list in French of the features that you think made it a good location for the Olympics.

Vocabulaire

montagneux/montagneuse   *mountainous*
plat(e)   *flat*

C. Report your group's findings to the class. Ask your teacher to list the results of these reports on the board: two combined lists of features—one for the Summer Games and one for the Winter Games.

3ᵉ Étape — Les jeux d'été ou les jeux d'hiver?

A. In your group, start your search for a Francophone city or town (and surrounding area) in which to hold *your* Olympic Games and research the climate and geography of your site. Would it be more suitable for the Winter or Summer Games? Perhaps your site is good for both games, only one, or neither **(ni l'un ni l'autre)**. Investigate each location, and record your answers in Part 4. If you discover your first choice is not suitable for any Olympics, select other sites until you locate a good one. Report your findings to the class.

B. As a class, vote on which Olympic Games you will organize and hold and where they will occur. Remember your Olympics will take place during the current season and at your location, so make reasonable choices. Record the class's decision under **Notre choix** on the same worksheet.

4ᵉ Étape   Qui fait quoi?

 This is your chance to decide which parts of organizing the Olympic Games you'd like to work on. Read through Committees Worksheet 5.A.2 for an overview of the project. Decide which committees you'd like to be part of and get together with the other interested students. You can be an athlete as well as work on one of the other committees, but you'll have to organize whatever else you do around the times when you're taking part in a game. Keep your worksheet(s) in your portfolio as you work through your part(s) of the games.

Les compétitions

As part of Committee B, it's up to you to decide what sporting events will be included in your games. You're going to design your own unique set of competitive events in which you and your classmates can participate.

Ressources utiles

■ Competitive Events Worksheets 5.B.1 and 5.B.2

■ Athlete Information Worksheet 5.E.1 (filled in)

■ Symbol Information Worksheet 5.F (filled in)

■ Poster board, strips of paper or cloth, glue or stapler, felt-tip marker

■ Computer with word-processing software

■ Portfolio

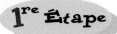

Créez les compétitions

A. Committee B needs to design the five or six games or contests that are appropriate for the Winter or Summer Games that your class is organizing. At least *one* of the contests must involve a result whose distance or height needs to be measured. At least *two* should require physical activity and *two* should not. Divide any additional games however you want.

Choose a partner and think about the kinds of games you like. You may use parts of different sports or board games that you know or invent totally new games. Perhaps you want a mixture of individual and team games, some with a lot of physical action and others with basically none. Some ideas follow:

Connexions

☑ Mathématiques
☑ Stratégies d'étude
☑ Technologie

• Can you set up your own **Tour de France** (or other kind of bike race) in the school parking lot or around the school track? How about a tricycle race?

- Did you enjoy those three-legged races from grade school?

- If someone has a set of **boules** or **pétanque** you could play a real French game. The Italian game of **bocce** uses the same equipment. And **boules** requires measurement!

- What about a board game that follows the same route as the auto race from Paris to Dakar?

Remember to keep in mind the information under **Notre choix** on Which Games? Worksheet 5.A.1 as you develop your games. The events will occur in the place and at the season described there. Use the prompts under Description of a Game on Competitive Events Worksheet 5.B.1 to guide your designs. With your partner, record your answers in English on a separate sheet of paper for each game you make.

B. Now form a whole group again and discuss the games each pair has invented. As you choose the games, keep in mind the requirements laid out in Activity A.

After you choose the games, calculate the total number of winners so that Committee D knows how many medals to make. Remember that each contest will have first-, second-, and third-place winners and each player on a winning team will receive a medal. Then divide up the work of gathering the necessary materials for playing the games and keeping score. (See **2ᵉ Étape** for creating a measuring tape.)

 C. Now members of Committee B may get together with the athletes (Committee E) and briefly describe the games. Be sure to state how many students are needed for each team in the team events. Next, write an explanation in English of how each one is played and scored.

To test whether the directions are clear, review them with the athletes. (Note: the word "athlete" refers to all competitors, whether they are participating in a game requiring physical activity or a board game.) You will know who the athletes in each game are because each one will give your committee a copy of Athlete Information Worksheet 5.E.1. Have the athletes practice each game and if the explanations are unclear, revise them. Write the final directions, a complete list of materials, and how the game is scored on Competitive Events Worksheet 5.B.2, which will be used at the games.

D. Give each game a name. At your Olympic Games, the names will be announced in French and, for any non-French speakers watching, in English. The name might indicate the action involved in the game (such as, Snowman Building—**Faire un bonhomme de neige,** Sandcastle Building—**Faire un château de sable**) or the number of people and the equipment the game requires (Two-Person Board Game—**Jeu de société pour deux personnes**). Record two of the French and English names on Competitive Events Worksheet 5.B.2. Finally, decide on the order in which the events will occur and write the numbers after Competition Number on the same worksheet.

To help the athletes practice, give them directions for the games in which they will compete. If a committee member wrote the directions on a computer, make multiple copies for your committee and the athletes.

E. Since the athletes at your games will all be speaking French, review the sports and games vocabulary in the Almanac. Brainstorm and add any phrases you think they may need to use while playing the games.

 F. Now that Committee B knows what the contests involve, talk with your teacher as a group about where to hold them. Can they be played in the classroom? Do they require gymnasium facilities or a track? When you know where each game will take place, add that information to Competitive Events Worksheet 5.B.2. Make and post signs to tell spectators when and where the various games are taking place.

2ᵉ Étape   Les distances

At international sporting competitions, distances are measured in meters rather than yards (1 meter = 1.094 yards). You can make your individual metric measuring tape by fastening together strips of paper or cloth and using a felt-tip pen to mark off 10-centimeter intervals (100 centimeters = 1 meter). A sample metric ruler is shown in the Almanac near the table of weights and measures. How many meters long does your tape need to be? Think about how far the athletes are likely to jump or how high they might build something.

3ᵉ Étape　Les rôles

As a committee, decide who will be the announcer and referee at the games. To allow as many students as possible on Committee B to participate at the games, change who plays these roles at each competitive event. Add this information to Competitive Events Worksheet 5.B.2.

- *Announcers:* The announcers tell the spectators in French a little about the athletes before each competition and announce the results. (Ask the athletes for their Athlete Information Worksheet 5.E.1. Ask the athletes' uniform designers for their Symbol Information Worksheet 5.F. You will use the information on these worksheets to introduce the athletes before they compete.) If the events at the actual games are held in different locations, be sure to include an announcement for the spectators about where the next competitive event will be held.

- *Referees:* The referees explain to the spectators in French how each game is played and scored. They supervise the game and take any necessary measurements. In addition, the referee keeps a record of each athlete's or team's score and gives that information to the announcer for Committee B. At the games, the referee will also tell the announcer for the Medal Committee the names of the first- (gold), second- (silver), and third-place (bronze) winners.

La cérémonie d'ouverture

The Olympic Games begin and end with special ceremonies. These entertaining ceremonies include the parade of athletes, speeches, and performances that reflect the culture of the host country. Committee C is going to design the opening ceremony for your mini-Olympics.

Ressources utiles

- Guidebooks for French-speaking countries and regions
- Books on Francophone customs, traditions, and legends
- Recordings of Francophone music
- Competitive Events Worksheet 5.B.2 (filled in)
- Opening Ceremony Worksheets 5.C.1 and 5.C.2
- National Team Worksheet 5.E.2 (filled in)
- Portfolio

1re Étape

Décrivez des cérémonies

As Committee C, discuss Olympic Game opening and closing ceremonies you have watched. Use the **Vocabulaire** box at the top of page 84 to help you speak French as much as possible. What happens at the ceremonies? What props are used?

Connexions

☑ Art
☑ Histoire
☑ Musique

Vocabulaire

chanter une chanson	*to sing a song*
danser	*to dance*
défiler dans	*to march into*
porter un drapeau	*to carry a flag*
le stade	*stadium*
tenir un discours	*to give a speech*

2ᵉ Étape — Fêtes, coutumes et légendes

A. Individually, use some of the materials listed in the **Ressources utiles** box to research celebrations, customs, or legends of the French-speaking host site that can be performed or enacted at the opening of the Games. Record your findings in Part 1 of Worksheet 5.C.1.

B. Report your findings to Committee C, describing as much of the custom, celebration, or legend as you can in French.

3ᵉ Étape — Quels talents avez-vous?

Make a list in French of all the talents you have in your committee. For example, who dances, sings, plays an instrument, draws, or speaks well in public? How can you combine the group's talents with a custom, celebration, or legend to make a special event that will be performed at the opening ceremony? Determine who will perform the special event. Record your decisions under The Performance at the Opening Ceremonies on Worksheet 5.C.1.

4ᵉ Étape — Où, comment et qui?

As Committee C, decide how you want to organize the ceremony and where you will need to hold it. Will you require electrical outlets for plugging in a CD or cassette player? If a dance is part of the performance, can the dance be done outside on the school grounds? How long will the ceremony be? When will the athletes parade in? In what order? When will the performance take place? Discuss your decisions with your teacher so that he or she can arrange an appropriate space for the ceremony.

Now use Opening Ceremony Worksheet 5.C.2 to list Committee C's tasks in French. Decide who will work on each one and record the names.

Record the order of the opening ceremony events in French on Opening Ceremony Worksheet 5.C.2. Then, in Part 3 list the order in which the national and regional teams will march in the parade.

5ᵉ Étape Au travail!

Now that your group has an idea of what the ceremonies will include and what your roles are, you need to work on the preparations, consulting with one another as you progress.

- *Speech writers:* Keep the opening speech brief and in French. Announce the various parts of the ceremony, such as the parade of athletes and the performance. To announce the parade, you need the names of the countries and regions represented at the games from Committee E. Also prepare a brief description of the performance. Find out from Committee B where the competitive events will be held, the name of each game, and the order in which the games will be played. Include this information at the appropriate time in the remarks.

- *Announcers:* Practice your speech and the announcements.

- *Performers*: What music, costumes, or props do you need? Plan and practice your performance.

- *Organizers:* Help everyone get organized in the parade.

- *Ushers*: Be prepared to direct spectators and athletes to their seats. Find out from the athletes what countries they represent and prepare a name sign for each country. On the day of the games, display signs that show where the athletes should sit. Prepare signs for spectator seating.

Once all preparations are made, hold a rehearsal to make sure everyone knows what he or she is supposed to do and when. For rehearsal purposes, members of your group should role-play the parts of the athletes and spectators.

Un peu plus

Write a theme song in French for your games! Or choose a piece of classical, folk, or pop music, preferably from the host country or region. If necessary, the music could be from a different French-speaking country or region.

La remise des médailles

A moving moment of every Olympic event is when the officials place the gold, silver, and bronze medals around the necks of the winners. The design for Olympic medals is determined by the country hosting the games and may reflect the history, geography, or culture of that country. You're going to design the medals and the awards ceremony for your Olympic Games.

Ressources utiles

- Books about Francophone history
- Books about the Olympic Games
- Colored markers, pencils, or paints; cardboard or poster board; scissors
- Competitive Events Worksheet 5.B.2 (filled in)
- Medals Worksheet 5.D.1
- Medals Ceremony Worksheet 5.D.2
- National Team Worksheet 5.E.2 (filled in)
- Computer with drawing software
- Portfolio

1ʳᵉ Étape **À quoi ressemble une médaille Olympique?**

Working with the other members of Committee D, locate at least one picture or description of an Olympic medal. Use some of the materials listed in the **Ressources utiles** box. Note the games that the medal is from (the season, place, and year), its shape, and the words, images, and designs on it. Record the information in Part 1 of Medals Worksheet 5.D.1.

Connexions

☑ Art
☑ Histoire
☑ Musique
☑ Technologie

2ᵉ Étape — Créez vos médailles

A. Now it's time to individually design your own set of three medals. Decide on the shape and size. Measurements should be metric. You can use the metric ruler near the table of weights and measures in the Almanac. What words, images, or designs will be on each medal? Perhaps you want to include a well-known geographic feature or a historic place, event, or person on the medal. Will you hang the medals from chains, ribbons, or strings? Record your decisions for each medal in Part 2 of Medals Worksheet 5.D.1.

B. Present your design to Committee D, describing it in French. After all group members have presented their ideas, decide which design(s) will be used for your games.

C. It's time to make the medals. Find out from Committee B how many winners you can expect. If any of the games are team events, find out how many people are on each team so you can prepare a medal for each team member. Record the information in Part 3 of Medals Worksheet 5.D.1.

3ᵉ Étape — Préparez la remise des médailles

As a committee, determine who will award the medals at the games. You may want a different presenter **(le présentateur/la présentatrice)** for each game. The presenter(s) should be sure to get the winners' names and countries from the referees (see Committee B) at the games. Each presenter should prepare a short speech that he or she can use when awarding the medals and congratulating the winners. As a presenter, record your basic speech on Medals Ceremony Worksheet 5.D.2, leaving out the information about the athlete's (or team's) name and country or region until the actual games.

4ᵉ Étape La répétition générale

Once the medals and speeches are ready, rehearse the ceremony with members of your committee role-playing the winners. Check with students working on Committee F to be sure they have the national anthems ready. They will be responsible for playing them at the ceremonies. If possible, have them participate in your rehearsal.

Vocabulaire

les médailles	*the medals*
la médaille Olympique	*Olympic medal*
remettre une médaille	*to give a medal*
C'est rond(e)/oval(e).	*It's round/oval.*
C'est en forme de cercle/triangle.	*It's in the shape of a circle/triangle.*
la cérémonie	*the ceremony*
Mesdames et Messieurs	*Ladies and Gentlemen*
La médaille d'or/d'argent/de bronze est attribuée à [*name of student*], gagnant(e) de/d' [*name of competition*].	*The gold/silver/bronze medal is going to ___, winner of the ___.*
Félicitations!	*Congratulations!*

Saviez-vous que ...?

In 1992 the French wanted the Summer Olympic Games held in Paris to honor the 100th anniversary of Pierre de Coubertin's first statement promoting the restoration of the Olympic Games. Instead they took place in Barcelona. To make up for this disappointment, **le Comité International Olympique (C.I.O.)** chose Albertville in the **département de Savoie** for the Winter Olympics. Jean-Claude Killy, a Frenchman who took all the gold medals in Alpine skiing at the 1968 Winter Games in Grenoble, France, was part of the International Olympic Committee helping to organize **les jeux d'hiver** in France.

Les athlètes

For athletes all over the world, competing in the Olympic Games is a great honor. On this committee, you are going to find out what the competitive events are, choose your contests, and practice for the games. You are also going to determine what Francophone region you will represent and will make a flag (alone or with teammates) to carry in the opening ceremony.

Ressources utiles

- World atlas
- Competitive Events Worksheets 5.B.1 and 5.B.2 (filled in)
- Opening Ceremony Worksheet 5.C.2 (filled in)
- Athlete Information Worksheet 5.E.1
- National Team Worksheet 5.E.2
- Paper, colored pencils, pens, or paints; ruler
- Guidebooks about French-speaking cities and towns
- A photo of yourself
- Portfolio
- The World Wide Web

1ʳᵉ Étape ## À quelles compétitions participez-vous?

A. Ask classmates on Committee B to present to your group the Olympic sporting events they've designed. Choose the event(s) in which you personally want to compete. Then in Committee E, arrange for the athletes who are taking part in team events to get together and form teams. Each team will represent a specific Francophone country or region.

Connexions

☑ Art
☑ Géographie
☑ Technologie

B. Committee B will ask you, as an individual and/or team member, to practice the games you are competing in to make sure the directions are clear. Once the committee has corrected any problems, you will get copies of the directions for the games. You can practice them on your own, with teammates, or with fellow competitors. Use the French vocabulary and phrases in the sports and games section of the Almanac as you do so.

2ᵉ Étape D'où venez-vous?

A. As an individual athlete or as a team, decide which French-speaking country or region you represent. Next, group yourselves according to geographic areas. Using guidebooks and maps, individually select your hometown. Find out its population and one other interesting fact. If more than one athlete wants the same hometown, only one should include its population as part of the researched information. The other athlete(s) should look for two additional facts about it. Write your name and this information on your own Athlete Information Worksheet 5.E.1.

Next, meet as national teams and complete National Team Worksheet 5.E.2 in French. Also have athletes who are participating as individuals record information about themselves in Part 3. Committee F needs this information in order to make your uniforms. You'll need to get your uniforms from them for the opening ceremonies and the games.

Explorons le Web!

Using the Country guide or Travel section of a Web guide, look for the population and other interesting facts about "your" town or city on the Web. You might also want to use the Reference section of a Web guide and look for information in an encyclopedia. The keyword would be the name of the city or town.

B. During sporting events, information is often given about the contestants. Complete the rest of Athlete Information Worksheet 5.E.1 in French so that the announcers will have information to pass along to the spectators.

Un @ peu plus

Write a short paragraph in French describing yourself for a press release. Include your age, where you're from, your hobbies, your favorite school subject, and your favorite food. Attach a photo to your description. With your group, display these paragraphs and photos in the classroom so that your fellow classmates can read up on the athletes who will be participating in the games.

Saviez-vous que ...?

From childhood, Pierre de Coubertin rode horseback, swam, rowed, played tennis, and biked. He believed in the importance of physical exercise, and he worked to make physical education as important as other courses in French education. Coubertin thought that he could partially use the Olympic Games to make physical exercise popular. Here is his famous statement describing what was necessary to get people involved in sports: To get 100 people involved in sports, you have to have 50 playing sports; to get 50 people playing sports, you have to have 20 dedicating themselves to sports; to get 20 people to dedicate themselves to sports, you have to have 5 who have amazing skills.

3e Étape   Les drapeaux

When Olympic athletes parade in the opening and closing ceremonies, one athlete from each country carries its flag. By obtaining a copy of Opening Ceremony Worksheet 5.C.2, you can learn where your country or region will march in the opening parade. Whether there is one person or several from the area that you're representing, find a picture of its flag. As a national team, decide who will make your flag and carry it in the opening ceremony. Then, using the picture you have found as a guide and some of the materials listed in the **Ressources utiles** box, the selected athlete(s) will make the flag and attach it to a ruler. One very lucky athlete will carry it in the opening ceremony.

Les costumes et les hymnes nationaux

In the opening and closing ceremonies, the Olympic athletes from a country or region wear similar clothing that often reflects their country or culture in some way. You're going to put together very simple costumes for the countries and regions represented by the athletes at your games.

Ressources utiles

- Books, magazines, and newspapers with Francophone information and pictures
- Materials for making costumes or symbol cards
- Recordings of national anthems of the French-speaking countries and folk songs or popular music of regions
- Competitive Events Worksheet 5.B.2 (filled in)
- National Team Worksheet 5.E.2 (filled in)
- Symbol Information Worksheet 5.F
- Portfolio
- Cassette player or CD player with speakers
- Computer with drawing software

1re Étape

Que portent les athlètes?

A. In your group as Committee F, get a copy of National Team Worksheet 5.E.2 from Committee E. Decide which athlete(s) each of you will design a costume or symbol card for. On your own, list each athlete's name, hometown, country, and the games in which he or she will take part on Symbol Information Worksheet 5.F.

Connexions

 Art
 Histoire
☑ Musique
☑ Stratégies
   d'étude

B. Continue on your own. Use the materials listed in the **Ressources utiles** box or textbooks to research costumes or symbols that you think may reflect the area(s) from which your athlete(s) come. For example, if your athlete(s) are from **Tahiti,** you may think that a palm tree with a beautiful beach is a typical symbol for this French overseas territory. Record the information on Symbol Worksheet 5.F.

C. For each country or region that you chose, design a simple costume or hanging card that your athlete(s) can wear. It should reflect your research. At the games, be sure to give the card(s) to your athlete(s).

 D. For each of your athletes, supply the information requested about your symbol in French on Symbol Information Worksheet 5.F. Use the **Vocabulaire** in Section D for help. Explain the meaning of the symbol in English and give the worksheet to the announcer on Committee B.

Un peu plus

Explain the meaning of the symbol in French. Have the announcer at the games use the French instead of the English version.

2ᵉ Étape   Les hymnes nationaux

When the medals are awarded at the Olympics, the national anthem or regional music of the gold medalist is played.

A. With your committee, locate a copy of the national anthem or regional music for each French-speaking country and region represented at your games. The French Department, the school library, or the town library may have the music you need. If you cannot find a particular piece, e-mail or write to the cultural attaché of the country's embassy nearest you. Explain in English why you need the music and express your thanks for any help the person is able to give you.

B. If you're not able to find a recording of a country's national anthem or an area's regional music, locate and use a piece of music by a composer or musician born in the country.

C. Consult with Committee D about when you'll play the national anthems or regional music at the awards ceremonies.

Les jeux sont ouverts

The big day is close at hand. To be sure everything is ready and that everyone knows how the games will proceed, you will have a dress rehearsal before holding the actual games.

Ressources utiles

- All props, costumes, game equipment, music, and so on from Committees B–F
- Games Schedule Worksheet 5.G
- Computer with word-processing software
- Portfolio (three-ring binder with pockets, file jacket, or file folder)

1re Étape — Est-ce que tout est prêt?

A. With your class, brainstorm a simple checklist in French of the preparations you have made for your Olympics. For example, the first items might be **Les compétitions** and **Informer les athlètes.** They indicate first that Committee B has designed the competitive events and has collected all the equipment. Committee B has also let the athletes know what the events are and what language they will need to use while participating.

B. Now each committee needs to check that it has obtained any information, props, and so forth needed from other committees.

2e Étape — Le programme

As a class, prepare a list in French of what will happen and when it will happen at the games. To be sure that nothing is left out, use the list of preparations from the **1re Étape** and the phrases at the top of Games Schedule Worksheet 5.G for help. Record the final list on the same worksheet.

Connexions

☑ Histoire
☑ Musique

3ᵉ Étape   Répétition générale!

Run through a rehearsal of the games, using your Games Schedule Worksheet 5.G as a guide. Because it is just a rehearsal, you may not wish to play each of the competitive events to completion. Rework or adjust any part of the games that isn't running smoothly.

4ᵉ Étape   Que les jeux commencent!

The big day is finally here. Hold the games. Good luck and have fun!

Un peu plus

The Olympic Games have something for everyone—from the sportsmanship of those competing, to the artistic talent of those designing medals, to the organizational ability of those overseeing the games as a whole. Now write and produce a short newsletter about your Olympics.

In your group, write a short article in French about your part in the Olympics—for example, how the design of the athletes' clothing reflects their countries.

If you have worked on more than one committee, choose your favorite to write about. Remember to give your article a headline. Ask your teacher to review your article. Then as a class, assemble your newspaper. Your teacher will distribute it to the other French classes at your school.

Présentez votre lycée

F or this project, you and your group are going to create a school guidebook (**un guide**) to be used by French-speaking exchange students. In the process, you will:

- Create a map of your school and label rooms, important features, and classroom items in French
- Prepare a profile of your school
- Present some of the extracurricular activities at your school
- Create a schedule of a typical day at your school
- Describe your school mascot (or create a new one) and invent a school cheer
- Design a school flag
- Videotape a guided tour of your school
- Create a title page and a table of contents to complete your school guidebook

Venez voir notre lycée!

Connexions

In the process of creating your school guidebook, you'll sharpen your skills in many areas.

- ✔ Art
- ✔ Géographie
- ✔ Histoire
- ✔ Mathématiques
- ✔ Médias

- ✔ Musique
- ☐ Santé et nutrition
- ☐ Sciences
- ✔ Stratégies d'étude
- ✔ Technologie

Look for the **Connexions** boxes throughout this project.

Warm-up: Avant de commencer ...

Before starting on your guidebook for French-speaking students, you'll need to do some brainstorming about your own school experience.

Ressources utiles

■ One three-ring binder per group with one pocket insert (or a 3-hole punched 9" x 13" manila envelope)

A. Form small groups. In your group, you can then each write three words in French that you associate with your school experience.

étudier   *sympathique*

le basket

B. Exchange papers with a partner. Now write down one word that you associate with each word your partner wrote.

étudier—beaucoup

sympathique—camarade

basket—sportif

C. Exchange papers with your partner again. Using the six words you now have on your paper, write one or two brief sentences about your school experience.

▶ Dans mon lycée, on étudie beaucoup.
Notre équipe de basket gagne tous ses matchs.
Mes camarades sont très sympathiques.

D. Share your sentences with your group.

E. As you complete each part of this project with your group, you'll be creating material for your group's school guidebook. Place your sentences in your group's binder.

Le lycée

For the first few days, it may be hard for new French-speaking students to find their way around your school. Drawing a map is the perfect way to help them out!

Ressources utiles

- French-English dictionary
- Colored pencils or markers
- 3" x 5" (or 5" x 7") blank index cards

1re Étape   ## Un plan du lycée

A. Working in a small group, draw a map of your school and the surrounding grounds. Your map needs to be large enough to accommodate small labels. If your school has more than one story, draw a floor plan for each story. If your student handbook has a map, adapt it for this project.

B. Work together to see how many rooms, offices, and other features you can label in French on your map. Then use your French textbook or a French-English dictionary to label any remaining features. Identify at least five classrooms by the names of the subjects taught in them.

C. Get together with another group and compare your maps. Have you forgotten anything important?

Connexions

☑ Art
☑ Stratégies
   d'étude

Saviez-vous que ...?

Can you guess what many university students in France consider a good job? Working as a **surveillant(e)** or **pion(ne)** (*monitor*) in a middle school (**un collège**). Many middle schools hire university students to supervise study halls (**les salles d'études**).

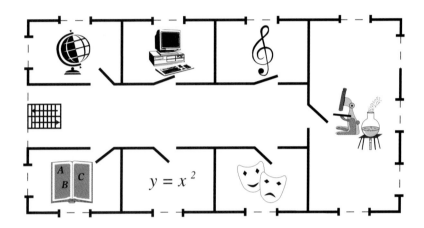

2ᵉ Étape Des fiches bilingues

A. Create bilingual flashcards to help the new students learn the names of some rooms, offices, and other features of your school. In your group, make eight flashcards with the French name on one side and the English on the other.

B. With your group, create eight more bilingual flashcards for items in your French classroom (desk, chair, bookcase, chalkboard, clock, and so forth).

3ᵉ Étape Préparez le guide

Put your group's school map into the guidebook binder. Place your group's flashcards in the pocket insert of the binder.

Des informations générales

A map provides a general picture of what your school looks like. A school profile, or an outline of different characteristics, can help new students see at a glance what life is like at your school.

Ressources utiles

■ Statistical information about your school

■ French-English dictionary

■ School Profile Worksheet 6.B

■ The World Wide Web

1re Étape   ## Les statistiques

Gather some basic statistics about your school.

 A. Answer the questions in Part 1 of School Profile Worksheet 6.B. Ask your school librarian, teachers, or administrators to help you find this information.

 B. In your group, compare your answers to Part 1 of Worksheet 6.B. If your answers differ, find out why. What sources did you each use? Then compare your answers with those of other groups.

Connexions

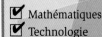

☑ Mathématiques
☑ Technologie

Explorons le Web!

If your school has its own Web site, look for the information there. Ask your teacher for the school's Web address, if you don't know it.

2ᵉ Étape   Les matières

In addition to a general overview, the new students will appreciate a guide to the specific subjects offered at your school.

A. As homework, create a chart like the one below.

Matière	Obligatoire?	Description
l'histoire américaine	oui	intéressante
les mathématiques	oui	facile
le chant	non	amusant

1. In the first column, list in French ten subjects at your school that you have taken or will take. Turn to the Almanac for a list of courses and subjects.

2. In the second column, indicate whether or not you're required to take the subject this year (**oui** or **non**).

3. In the third column, write one adjective in French that you think best describes each subject.

B. In French, compare your chart with those of others in your group. Are all of your required subjects the same? How similar or different are your descriptions of the subjects? Are the descriptions positive?

Vocabulaire

Quels sont tes cours cette année (ce semestre)?	*What classes are you taking this year (semester)?*
J'ai un cours de/d'___.	*I'm taking ___.*
Comment est le cours de/d'___?	*What's ___ like?*
Est-ce qu'il est obligatoire?	*Is it required?*

C. In your group, divide the subjects you have listed in your charts into three categories: academic (**les matières académiques**), arts (**les matières artistiques**), and other subjects (**les autres matières**). Then list at least three subjects under each category in Part 2 of School Profile Worksheet 6.B. Include descriptions as well. Be positive! One member of your group should record an official list of the group's answers.

D. Add your group's School Profile Worksheet 6.B to your school guidebook.

Saviez-vous que...?

In France, the grading system is based on a 20-point scale. Generally, a grade (**une note**) between 0 and 10 is not passing (**insuffisant**), 11–15 is satisfactory (**satisfaisant**), and over 15 is excellent (**excellent**). It is very rare for anyone to receive 18–20 points. Students must have a year's average over 10 to go on to the next level. They have to repeat (**redoubler**) the entire year if they fail even *one* important class, such as math or French.

Les activités périscolaires

The French-speaking students may want to get involved in extracurricular activities. Introduce them to some of the organizations and teams at your school.

Ressources utiles

■ Extracurricular Activities Worksheet 6.C

1re Étape   Les sports

A. In your group, write a list in French of at least six sports teams or intramural sports your school has. Organize your list according to season (fall, winter, spring) on Extracurricular Activities Worksheet 6.C. Refer to your textbook and the list of sports in the Almanac.

B. Now make your own survey of five classmates in other groups to find out what their favorite school sports are. Report your findings to your group. On Extracurricular Activities Worksheet 6.C, record which sport is most popular among your classmates. One member of your group should record the group's answers.

2e Étape   Les associations et les clubs

A. As a group, find out which clubs and organizations various group members belong to. List them in French on Extracurricular Activities Worksheet 6.C. Next to each club or organization, write a brief description of it in French. Refer to the list of clubs and organizations in the Almanac.

Connexions

☑ Stratégies d'étude

B. Now get together with another group and exchange information. Add any new information to Extracurricular Activities Worksheet 6.C.

Vocabulaire

Tu es membre de quel club?	*What club are you a member of?*
Je suis membre du club de/d'___.	*I'm a member of the ___ club.*
Je suis membre d'une association bénévole.	*I'm a member of a volunteer organization.*
Qu'est-ce que tu fais au club de/d'___?	*What do you do in the ___ club?*
Je travaille sur l'annuaire.	*I work on the yearbook.*
le journal du lycée/collège	*school newspaper*
préparer	*to prepare*
organiser	*to organize*
aider	*to help*
réfléchir	*to think about*
pratiquer	*to practice*

 C. Add Extracurricular Activities Worksheet 6.C to your group's binder.

Saviez-vous que...?

Extracurricular sports activities are not common in the French schools. Generally each town has a few teams (soccer, basketball, gymnastics) that compete in regional or national competitions. Schools don't always have a gymnasium, but use town facilities for physical education classes (**l'éducation physique et sportive**)—**EPS** (pronounced like the letters of the alphabet). When going to gym class, students say **Je vais au sport** or **Je vais à l'EPS**.

D Une journée typique

elp the French-speaking students experience a typical day of classes at your school. Assist them with schedules and directions.

Ressources utiles

■ School map from Section A

1re Étape ## L'emploi du temps

A. Create a chart with the days of the week in French across the top and the times corresponding to your class periods down the left side.

B. Create a model schedule for new students at your school by filling in the chart in French with your own school schedule. Add room numbers to indicate where the class meets.

Saviez-vous que ...?

In France, many small towns and rural areas do not have a local high school, so students must go to larger nearby towns to attend high school. As a result, some teenage students live in boarding houses during the week so they can go to high school. School buses are provided for elementary school children, but not for high school students. Students who live in cities take public transportation—buses or the subway—to school.

Connexions

☑ Géographie
☑ Stratégies
  d'étude

2ᵉ Étape　Où est ... ?

A. Now help students find their way from one class to the next. Using your schedule and your group's school map, write directions in French so that the new students could find their way from:

- the main entrance to your first class
- your first class to your second class
- the cafeteria to your first class after lunch
- one class to any other class on your schedule

▶ Pour aller de la cantine à la classe d'algèbre dans la salle 207:
　Tourne à droite.
　Va tout droit jusqu'au gymnase.
　Au gymnase, tourne à gauche.
　Monte l'escalier.
　L'algèbre est dans la troisième salle à gauche (207).

B. Work in pairs. Give one set of your directions to your partner, who will trace the route you describe on a school map. Reverse roles. Are your partner's directions accurate? Are yours accurate?

Vocabulaire

à droite/à gauche	*to the right/to the left*
marcher	*to walk*
jusqu'au/à la/à l'/aux [+ *noun*]	*until, to the* [+ *noun*]
l'escalier (*m.*)	*(flight of) stairs*
le couloir	*hallway*
monter/descendre l'escalier	*to go up/go down the stairs*
tourner	*to turn*
tout droit	*straight ahead*
traverser	*to cross*

C. Put your schedule and directions into your group's binder as samples for the visitors.

L'esprit scolaire

Students have many ways of expressing their school spirit. At a football game, for example, there may be a school mascot that represents the team. The cheerleaders try to inspire the crowd and support the athletes. Help the new French-speaking students catch your school spirit!

Ressources utiles

■ Colored markers
■ French-English dictionary

Vocabulaire

l'équipe (*f.*)	*team*
le fan, le supporter	*fan*
le hourra, le bravo	*cheer*
la mascotte	*mascot*
encourager, supporter	*to cheer, to support*
Vive [+ *singular noun*]!	*Long live ___ !*
Vive notre lycée!	*Long live our high school!*
Vivent [+ *plural noun*]!	*Long live ___ !*
Vivent les Tigres!	*Long live the Tigers!*
Allez les Tigres!	*Go Tigers!*

Connexions

 Art
 Musique

1re Étape   La mascotte

In your group, draw your school mascot and describe it in French. Use your current school mascot or create one of your own. Then present your mascot to the class.

▶ Notre mascotte est le tigre. Le tigre est grand et beau. Il est jaune avec des rayures noires ...

Un peu plus

How does your mascot represent your school? With your group, write a sentence in French that describes both your mascot and your school.

▶ Le tigre et mon lycée sont tous les deux forts, grands, intelligents ...

Saviez-vous que ...?

The most famous French cheer is «**Allez les bleus!**». It is used for the French national soccer team because the team uniforms are blue and white.

The soccer team's mascot is a rooster. Why a rooster? The rooster is a symbol for France, especially in sporting events. The rooster represents energy, willingness to play aggressively, and determination to win.

The rooster has been one of the symbols of France ever since the days of Julius Caesar, when France was called **la Gaule**. By coincidence, the Latin word *gallus* meant both "Gaul" and "rooster."

2e Étape   Hourra!

A. In your group, decide whether you're going to write a cheer for your whole school or for one team or organization at your school. Then brainstorm action verbs in French related to your school, your team or organization, or your mascot. For example, if your mascot is a tiger, you might come up with verbs such as **courir** or **sauter**.

B. Now brainstorm some adjectives that describe your school, your team or organization, or your mascot. For example, **rapide**, **fort**, and **dangereux** are adjectives that might describe a tiger. One member of your group should record the group's ideas.

C. Finally, combine some of the verbs and adjectives you brainstormed into a simple but energetic school cheer, such as the one shown. Have your teacher review your group's cheer. Then teach it to the rest of the class.

Vite les Tigres, vite!
Courez les Tigres, courez!
Forts les Tigres, forts!
Courez, jouez, gagnez!

D. Add your school cheer and the picture and information about your mascot to your school guidebook.

Le drapeau

Countries, states, schools, and organizations are often represented by a flag or banner. The colors and designs on these flags are usually carefully chosen to symbolize the ideals of the groups they represent.

Ressources utiles

- An encyclopedia or almanac
- Colored markers
- Construction paper
- The World Wide Web

1ʳᵉ Étape   ## Le drapeau des États-Unis

As a class, discuss the significance of the symbols and colors of the U.S. flag.

1. Quelles sont les trois couleurs du drapeau des États-Unis?

2. Est-ce que ces couleurs sont importantes? Qu'est-ce qu'elles représentent?

3. Combien d'étoiles y a-t-il sur le drapeau? Pourquoi?

Saviez-vous que ...?

In most Francophone countries people don't hang flags inside or outside their homes, and schools usually don't display the flag either; such actions would be considered extreme. Flags appear on government buildings only on national holidays and for special events.

Connexions

- ☑ Art
- ☑ Géographie
- ☑ Histoire
- ☑ Technologie

2e Étape — Les drapeaux du monde francophone

Working with your group, look at an encyclopedia or your French text-book and select the flag of one French-speaking country. List in French the colors and symbols on the flag. What values or history do you think the colors and symbols might represent? Discuss your ideas in English. Consult an encyclopedia to find more information about the flag you chose. How does this information compare with your own ideas about the flag? Present your findings to the class in English.

Explorons le Web!

To get more information about the flag you've chosen, search the World Wide Web using a Web guide.

Keywords

"flags of the world"

3e Étape — Créez un drapeau

A. Create a flag for your school or town. With your group, make a list in French of colors that you might want to include on your school flag. Next to each color, write what it would represent. You could include your school colors and perhaps add one or two more.

▶ le blanc = la vérité
le doré = l'excellence

les rayures (*f. pl.*)

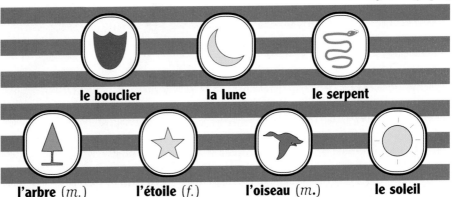

| le bouclier | la lune | le serpent |

| l'arbre (*m.*) | l'étoile (*f.*) | l'oiseau (*m.*) | le soleil |

B. Now draw some symbols that you think would represent your school. Next to each symbol, write in French what it stands for. You could include your school mascot or an important feature of your town or school. Use your imagination!

▶ le tigre = la force
les étoiles = l'ambition

C. Using your lists of colors and symbols, draw your flag or make it out of construction paper.

Write a brief explanation in French of the colors and symbols on your flag and how they represent your school or town.

▶ Notre drapeau a deux couleurs. Le blanc représente la vérité. Le doré représente l'excellence académique. Au centre du drapeau il y a une étoile. L'étoile représente l'ambition parce que les élèves ici travaillent beaucoup.

4ᵉ Étape   Préparez le guide

Explain your flag to the class. Display your flag in the classroom. Create a small version of your flag and add it to your group's school guidebook, along with your description of its colors and symbols.

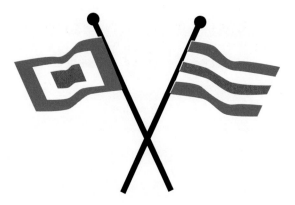

La visite guidée

Schools and towns attract students or residents by providing colorful informational brochures, videotapes, or even CD-ROMs about their schools and community facilities. Introduce the new French-speaking students to your school by videotaping your own guided tour.

Ressources utiles

- School map from Section A
- French-English dictionary
- Video camera and blank videotape
- Construction paper, poster board, or colored paper
- Heavy-duty elastic band
- Computer with word-processing program

1re Étape — Les décisions

A. With your group, review the map you made of your school and school grounds in Section A. Make a list of the rooms, offices, and features of the school that should be shown in your video tour.

B. Consulting your teacher, find two teachers willing to appear in your video. Teach them each a short greeting in French (for example, **Bonjour** or **Bienvenue au cours de mathématiques**).

Connexions

 Médias
✔ Technologie

2ᵉ Étape Les commentaires

Working with your group, write one or two sentences in French to introduce and describe each of the teachers, rooms, and features you've chosen to highlight in your video. For each, consider what significance it has for your school. Are there any relevant facts or statistics you can share? For example, how long has the biology teacher been at your school? When was the computer lab opened?

▶ Madame Lundgren enseigne au lycée depuis dix ans.
La salle d'informatique est neuve.
Notre équipe de gymnastique est la meilleure de l'état.

Un peu plus

Find someone in your school (other than your French teacher!) who speaks French. Videotape a brief interview in French with him or her. You might ask for some advice for the new students.

3ᵉ Étape — Les détails de la production

A. With your group, plot the route you will take in taping your video tour. Use the descriptions you wrote in the **2ᵉ Étape** to put together a short script in French for your video. Have the students in your group introduce themselves at the beginning of the tour.

B. Decide how you will divide up the roles of director, narrator, and camera operator. You may want to share a role or change roles with each new scene.

C. Create the title and credits for your video tour using construction paper or poster board or use attractive fonts from a word-processing program and print them out on colored paper.

4ᵉ Étape — Action!

Finally, you're ready to tape the video tour of your school. It should be about three to five minutes long. All of the narration should be done in French. Remember to speak clearly! Rehearse your tour at least once before you begin taping. When your video tour is complete, show it to your class; then include it in your completed school guidebook along with your script. Use a heavy-duty elastic band to "attach" your video to your guidebook.

Les derniers détails

To complete your school guidebook, make it easy to use by adding a title page, table of contents, and page numbers.

Ressources utiles

- School guidebook binder
- Construction paper and colored markers
- Computer with word-processing program

1re Étape — La page de présentation

In your group, create a title page for your school guidebook using colored markers and construction paper or a computer word-processing program. Include the following useful information:

- Name, address, and phone number of your school

- Your group members' names and the date

- Other names, phone numbers, and office numbers that new students may need (the school nurse, principal, guidance counselor, and so on)

Saviez-vous que ...?

In France, the country is divided into three educational zones. All students in the same zone have winter and spring holidays at the same time, and the times differ slightly from zone to zone. The school day often runs until 4:00 or 5:00 P.M. Students stay in the same classroom all day, except for classes that require special setups, such as laboratory science, art, or gym. Teachers travel from room to room.

Connexions

☑ Art
☑ Technologie

2ᵉ Étape — La table des matières

Make a table of contents. Assign each item in your guidebook a page number so that new students will be able to locate the information quickly and easily. On a separate sheet of paper, list each item in your school guidebook and add page numbers.

3ᵉ Étape — Et voilà!

Insert your title page and contents page into the front of your school guidebook binder. Congratulations on a job well done!

Organisez un défilé de mode

Using your knowledge of clothing and French cultures, you and your group will produce a fashion show. In the process, you will:

- Find examples of what French teenagers are wearing and compare styles of American and French clothing
- Set up your own fashion design house
- Take on different roles for the preparation of the show
- Make a program and advertisement for the show
- Add decoration and music to the show
- Hold the fashion show

À vos ciseaux!

Connexions

As you create your fashion show, you will sharpen your skills in many areas.

☑ Art	☑ Musique
☐ Géographie	☐ Santé et nutrition
☐ Histoire	☐ Sciences
☐ Mathématiques	☑ Stratégies d'étude
☑ Médias	☑ Technologie

Look for the **Connexions** boxes throughout this project.

Warm-up: Parlons de la mode!

D
o you want to use your imagination and have some fun? You are going to be a fashion designer and present your unique creations at a show. Your clothing and accessories can show your interests, the kind of person you are, or just be for fun. Let's get started by talking about what you like to wear and where you like to shop.

Vocabulaire

Est-ce que ___ te plaît/plaisent?	*Do you like ___?*
(À) moi non plus.	*Me neither.*
porter	*to wear*
l'affaire (*f.*)	*bargain*
la marque	*brand, name*
la boutique	*shop (small)*
le centre commercial	*mall*
la grande surface	*superstore*
le magasin de vêtements	*clothing store*
le magasin de vêtements d'occasion	*second-hand clothing store*
la vente par correspondance	*mail-order shopping*
le catalogue	*catalog*
la revue, le magazine de mode	*fashion magazine*
la vitrine	*shop window*
faire du lèche-vitrines	*to go window shopping*
les soldes (*m. pl.*)	*sales*
en solde	*on sale*

A. Do you prefer comfortable clothes? Do you like the latest fashions? In a small group, discuss in French the kinds of clothes and accessories you prefer to wear. Here are a few sentences to get you started.

▶ Quel type de vêtements est-ce que tu aimes porter?
Je préfère les vêtements confortables.
Les robes ne me plaisent pas.
Je m'habille à la mode.

Saviez-vous que ...?

Levi Strauss, a tailor by trade, went to California to make his fortune in the 1849 gold rush. He didn't find gold, but he did notice that miners needed heavy-duty clothing. Strauss started making clothing from the canvas used for tents. Then he discovered a new, less bulky cloth that came from Nimes (**de Nîmes**), in France. It was perfect for the work clothes he was making. This material became known as *denim*.

B. Where do you usually shop for clothes? in department stores? discount stores? clothing stores? through catalogs? In a small group, talk in French about your shopping habits.

▶ —Où est-ce que tu achètes tes vêtements?
—J'achète mes vêtements dans les boutiques. Et toi?

C. Do you look at clothing ads? Where are you likely to look for the kind of clothes you like? In a newspaper, a special magazine, or elsewhere? In your small group, continue talking in French about your shopping habits.

▶ —Je cherche des vêtements dans des revues de mode comme *Elle*.
—Je fais du lèche-vitrines.

Les adolescents et la mode

Traditionally clothing styles came from Europe and then became popular in the U.S. Like many other businesses, however, fashion is now more international. Since World War II, the U.S. has become more and more influential in fashion. You know what U.S. teenagers wear, but what about French teenagers? Investigate the fashions in the French-speaking world.

Ressources utiles

- Clothing Comparison Worksheet 7.A
- French magazines (Some, such as *Elle* and *Marie Claire,* are published in both French and English.)
- Catalogs from French mail-order businesses, such as *La Redoute*
- French-English dictionary
- The World Wide Web
- A folder to compile your worksheets and materials for this project

1ʳᵉ Étape — Qu'est-ce que les adolescents portent?

Individually or in pairs, use some of the items listed in the **Ressources utiles** box to determine what French teenagers are wearing. Remember to consider as many French-speaking countries or regions as you wish! Then complete the information in Part 1 of Clothing Comparison Worksheet 7.A.

Connxions

 Médias
 Technologie

Explorons le Web!

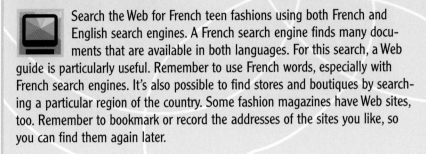

Search the Web for French teen fashions using both French and English search engines. A French search engine finds many documents that are available in both languages. For this search, a Web guide is particularly useful. Remember to use French words, especially with French search engines. It's also possible to find stores and boutiques by searching a particular region of the country. Some fashion magazines have Web sites, too. Remember to bookmark or record the addresses of the sites you like, so you can find them again later.

Keywords

"Galeries Lafayette"
"haute couture"
"Guide de mode"
"Marie Claire"
Elle
magasin

Saviez-vous que ...?

Can you guess what **les pattes d'éléphant** are? (**Pattes** are the legs or paws of an animal and the feet of a bird.) Where the French see *elephant leg pants*, English-speakers see *bell-bottoms*. Now think about what pattern **les pattes de canard** describes. (**Canard** means *duck*.) This ragged pattern is *duck feet* in French, but *houndstooth* in English.

2ᵉ Étape — Comparez vos recherches!

In your group, discuss in French what you have discovered, answering the questions in Part 2 on Clothing Comparison Worksheet 7.A. How are French and American clothes alike or different? What are the most popular colors and types of clothing? Refer to the Almanac for clothing and colors.

▶ Les adolescentes américaines et françaises portent des jupes courtes.

Le violet foncé est à la mode en France. Le vert clair est à la mode aux États-Unis.

Les premiers pas

Before your fashions hit the runway, there are many decisions to make and many things to prepare. First, you'll need to decide the kind of clothing your group wants to create and present in the show. What about clothes of the future, or regional costumes, or simply casual clothes? You'll also have to decide how you want to present them.

Ressources utiles

▨ French-English dictionary

▨ Picture dictionary in French or multiple languages

▨ Fashion Show Decision Worksheet 7.B

▨ The World Wide Web

▨ Worksheet folder

1ʳᵉ Étape   Votre maison de couture

A. Fashion reflects a variety of styles and functions. In your group, think about and discuss in French the overall idea of your fashion collection. Use the questions and suggestions under **Les idées** on Fashion Show Decision Worksheet 7.B to come up with an outline of your collection. Be sure to record your decisions by checking the boxes or writing some additional ideas.

B. Fashion designers have to have a house name! What's yours going to be? Something unusual like **La maison grunge** or something very impressive like **La maison de mille étoiles?** Write the name of your fashion design house on Fashion Show Decision Worksheet 7.B.

Connexions

☑ Stratégies
   d'étude

2ᵉ Étape Décidez de l'organisation du défilé

Keeping in mind the decisions your design house made in the **1ʳᵉ Étape**, discuss as a class—in French—how to organize the show. Use the questions and suggestions under **L'organisation du défilé** on Fashion Show Decision Worksheet 7.B for help, and record your choices.

3ᵉ Étape Le nom du défilé

Next you need to choose a name for your fashion show. As a class, brainstorm names for the show. Vote for your favorite name and write your class's decision on Fashion Show Decision Worksheet 7.B. Put your worksheets in your folder.

Saviez-vous que...?

Haute couture (*high fashion*) refers to styles by designers such as Chanel, Dior, Givenchy, and Jean-Paul Gaultier—**les grands couturiers**. When a designer becomes very important, his or her business is called a "house," for example **la maison Dior**. Fashion houses introduce new styles in Paris twice a year—spring and summer fashions in January, and fall and winter fashions in July. These shows are called a collection, for example, **la collection automne/hiver 99**.

Au travail!

Being a fashion designer means you have a chance to do different things. Everyone will help design and assemble the fashions. Modeling, writing fashion descriptions, and so on, however, will be divided among group members to be sure that everything gets done. Keep the different choices in mind as you select what you want to do. You can't model and comment at the same time.

Ressources utiles

- Materials such as cardboard, construction paper, feathers, cloth, rope, ribbon, plastic, glue, markers, tape, staplers, scissors
- French newspapers, magazines, mail-order catalogs
- French-English and picture dictionaries
- Fashion Show Decision Worksheet 7.C
- Worksheet folder

1re Étape   Les créateurs et leurs créations

Now comes the fun part, making those fashions! Everyone in your fashion design house will work together to create them.

 A. Keep your fashion theme in mind as your fashion house brainstorms ideas for actual fashions in English. List the items you decide to create on Fashion Show Decision Worksheet 7.C. Then allow models to select what they will model. Write their names on Worksheet 7.C. You need to know who will wear each item so that you can make the clothes "fit." Finally, decide on the order in which your house will show its fashions and record the information on the worksheet.

Connexions
 Art

B. You may use all kinds of materials to make your fashions—paper, foil, or leather, for example. You may make an entire piece of clothing or add to an existing one. In your group, make a list of who will bring in which materials to make your fashions. There are more suggestions in the **Ressources utiles** box.

C. It's now time to actually create your collection. Don't forget to let the models try the outfits on before the show so you can make any necessary adjustments.

2ᵉ Étape — Les mannequins

At the same time you're creating your fashions, you need to decide who will be modeling them.

 A. Step right up! Who's ready to be a model, or a **mannequin**, as they call it in French? How can you resist the opportunity to wear some of these gorgeous new styles? On Fashion Show Decision Worksheet 7.C, write each model's name next to the item he or she will present.

B. Each model may wear one or more of the fashions during the show.

3ᵉ Étape — Les commentateurs

When designers bring their fashions to the runway, they do more than show their designs—they describe and comment on them as well. A vivid description of each model's outfit will help capture your audience's attention.

 A. In your fashion house group, divide the creations among pairs of students. On Worksheet 7.C, record who will comment on what item. In pairs, and using the materials listed in the **Ressources utiles** box, research how fashions are described. As you read, jot down expressions that you might want to use to talk about your own creations. Refer to the illustrations on the next page for ideas.

B. Then, work with your partner to answer these questions about each item you'll be describing.

1. Quel genre d'article de mode est-ce?

2. Comment s'appelle le mannequin qui présente l'article?

3. De quelle couleur est cet article?

4. En quel tissu est cet article?

5. Dans quelles situations est-ce qu'on porte cet article?

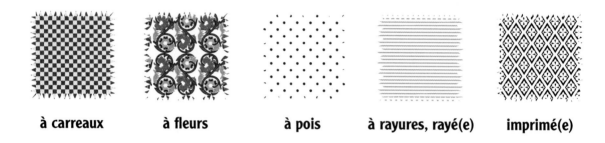

à carreaux   **à fleurs**   **à pois**   **à rayures, rayé(e)**   **imprimé(e)**

C. In pairs, write an introduction for each of your fashion(s), using the information above. The example below shows one way the information collected might introduce a model and the fashion he or she is wearing.

▶ Voici Alain.
Il aime jouer au foot.
Il porte un short rayé rouge et bleu.

Un peu plus

Expand the description by adding more details. The answers to these questions may help.

1. Quel temps fait-il quand on porte cet article?

2. En quelle saison est-ce qu'on porte cet article?

3. Pourquoi est-ce que cet article plaît au mannequin?

D. Practice reading or saying your part in the fashion show aloud.

Le programme et la publicité

rganizers of various kinds of shows often advertise their pro-
ductions. A program will then help the audience follow what's
happening. One half of the class will work on the Program
Committee, the other half on the Publicity Committee.

Ressources utiles

▨ Worksheets 7.B and 7.C

▨ Program and Publicity Worksheet 7.D

▨ Plain 8 ½" x 11" paper, poster board, and markers

▨ Newspapers and magazines that include clothing for teenagers

▨ Catalogs from French mail-order businesses

▨ French-English and picture dictionaries

▨ Worksheet folder

1re Étape   Qui invitez-vous au défilé?

As a class, discuss in French whom you want to invite to your fashion
show. Do you want to present your creations to other French classes,
families, teachers, and so on?

2e Étape   Le programme

A. In your Program Committee, brainstorm a list of all the information that should be included in the program. Check with your teacher
about your options for the place, date, and time of the fashion show
before listing this information. Remember that French speakers often
state time according to a 24-hour clock for events such as this.

Connexions

 Art
 Médias
 Technologie

B. Now complete the information in Part 1 of Program and Publicity Worksheet 7.D. The information on Fashion Show Decision Worksheets 7.B and 7.C will also help you. As you make decisions about the program, remember to:

- Plan what the cover will look like

- Determine who is responsible for keyboarding and duplicating the program

- Coordinate your information with the Publicity Committee

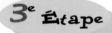

Vocabulaire

avoir lieu	*to take place*
fascinant(e)	*fascinating*
passionnant(e)	*exciting*
l'événement (*m.*)	*event*
le spectacle	*show*

3ᵉ Étape   La publicité

An important fashion show needs a good advertising campaign. It's time to get the word out! Decide how you want to advertise the fashion show—with flyers, through posters, or by some other means. If you want to use your school public address system or your school Intranet, read the suggestions in B and C on the next page.

 A. In your Publicity Committee, using materials listed in the **Ressources utiles** box on page 133, look for ads for various kinds of events—plays, concerts, and so forth. List the kinds of information these ads contain. Then discuss in French the information needed to advertise your show. Complete the information on Part 2 of Program and Publicity Worksheet 7.D. Jot down any English or French expressions that might help you write an ad. Make sure you coordinate your information with the Program Committee.

B. How about making a radio ad? If you have French-language radio stations in your area, listen to some of their ads. Otherwise, try ads on English-language radio stations. Decide how you're going to present the information in your ad—through the voice of one announcer? in the form of a conversation? Write, practice, and record your ad. Don't forget to use background sound effects!

C. If your school has an Intranet, use it as a quick way to get the word out about your fashion show. Since not everyone can read French, be sure to post your ad in English, too. Using the information you've gathered, write the details in both languages. Use descriptive words and/or art to make the ad more interesting. Before you send off the final copy, be sure to proofread it. Everyone in the whole school will read it!

Saviez-vous que ... ?

Clothing sizes in France differ from those in the U.S. Men's and women's shirts and sweaters are often marked 1, 2, and 3 for small, medium, and large. Although there are size conversion charts for items such as dresses, suits, slacks, and skirts, the sizes are only approximately the same. Shoes provide another challenge. Half-sizes and large sizes are hard to find. Shoes ordinarily do not come in different widths except orthopedic shoes and shoes for children. Refer to the size conversion chart in the Almanac.

Les derniers préparatifs

You're about to invest time and effort in the finishing touches that can make the difference between a good show and a great one—the music, the decorations, and a dress rehearsal to make sure everyone knows what to do.

Ressources utiles

▦ Poster board or plain butcher paper

▦ Art supplies such as markers and construction paper

▦ Musical instruments, music tapes, or CDs

▦ French-English dictionary

▦ Video camera or tape recorder and blank tapes

1re Étape Le maître de cérémonies

Next up is finding a master of ceremonies to open and close the show and to introduce each fashion design house. Select one of your classmates for this role. Then as a class, brainstorm what should be included in his or her speeches. The master of ceremonies will then finalize the text on his or her own.

2e Étape La musique

Connexions

☑ Art
☑ Médias
☑ Musique

Now form a Music Committee to select and list the music that you are going to play. Choose a committee member to tell the Program Committee what the music program will be. Arrange when and where you are going to rehearse. Be prepared to play the music during the dress rehearsal of the show.

3e Étape Les décorations

You will also need to form a Decorating Committee. Use your imagination and have fun. Try to coordinate the decorations with the fashions being presented. If it is necessary to change decorations during the show, be ready to practice this during the dress rehearsal.

4e Étape La répétition

It's almost time for the real thing, but first a rehearsal. There are many things to check out. Can the models present their fashions with the decorations in place? Are the fashions wearable? Is the music ready? Here's an opportunity to hear and improve your performance. Video-tape or tape-record the rehearsal so that the announcers and models hear their French. There's nothing like hearing and seeing yourself to know what you've got down pat and what needs a little more practice.

Enfin le jour du défilé

When you're preparing for a show, it seems as if the show will never happen. There are always more and more things to do, but **enfin le jour est arrivé**!

Ressources utiles

▨ French-English dictionary
▨ All the materials you made and gathered for the fashion show
▨ Worksheet folder

 1re Étape   ## Est-ce que tout est prêt?

As a class, make the final preparations for your show. Arrange the decorations and the furniture. Set out the programs. Make sure the music is ready and get into your designer clothes. Have copies of your speeches handy in case you need them. If you have more than one task, make sure everything is laid out so you can easily move from one to the other.

2e Étape   ## Ouvrez les portes!

If you have guests, seat them and hand out the programs. Ready, set, music! Enjoy the show!

Vocabulaire

Quel beau pull!	What a beautiful sweater!
Que c'est chouette, extra, super!	How great, terrific!
... démodé	. . . old-fashioned
... moche [ravissant]	. . . ugly [beautiful]
aller bien (*used with clothing*)	to look good
Ce manteau lui va bien.	This coat fits him/her well. This coat looks good on him/her.

3ᵉ Étape Les réactions du public

During a fashion show, the audience often comments on what they like and dislike. If you're part of the audience, you need to be able to express and exchange your opinions. Use some of the following questions to help you discuss the clothing at the fashion show.

• Comment trouves-tu [ce foulard]?

• Quel foulard préfères-tu? Le bleu? Le noir?

• Est-ce que tu achèterais [un short] comme ça?

Un peu plus

Take notes at the fashion show to expand into a newspaper review. Use what you have gathered throughout the project to help you. Pay attention to items such as these:

1. Quel est ton vêtement favori? Pourquoi?

2. Qu'est-ce qui ne te plaît pas? Pourquoi?

3. Que penses-tu des collections?

4. Pour toi, quelle est la meilleure partie du défilé?

5. As-tu remarqué quelque chose qui t'intéresse en particulier?

Passons à la météo...

Have you ever wanted to control the weather? Well, here's your chance! Using your knowledge of weather and French, you and your group will create a local cable news weather report for French-speaking visitors to the U.S. You can present it live or on video-tape. In the process, you will:

- Collect ideas from weather reports that you watch and read
- Write a local weather forecast covering several days and give temperatures in Celsius
- Create a weather map and other illustrations to accompany your forecast
- Stage a live, on-the-scene weather report
- Rehearse and present your weather forecast

On passe maintenant à la météo...

Connexions

In the process of making a weather report, you'll sharpen your skills in many areas.

- ✔ Art
- ✔ Géographie
- ☐ Histoire
- ✔ Mathématiques
- ✔ Médias

- ☐ Musique
- ☐ Santé et nutrition
- ✔ Sciences
- ✔ Stratégies d'étude
- ✔ Technologie

Look for the **Connexions** boxes throughout this project.

Warm-up: **Parlons de la pluie et du beau temps!**

> ## Ressources utiles
>
> - Climate and Weather Expressions Worksheet 8.W
> - Map of the U.S.
> - Portfolio (binder with pockets, a file jacket, or a file folder) for each student
> - The World Wide Web

A. Are you a person who is fascinated by the weather and follows forecasts closely? Or do you prefer to be surprised by the weather? As a class, brainstorm in English the times when the weather is important to you. List your ideas on the board.

 B. You know what your local climate is like, and you already know some weather expressions in French. As a class, brainstorm the French expressions you know. Record them on Climate and Weather Expressions Worksheet 8.W under Expressions I Know. Then think of other words and expressions in English that you could use to describe your local weather. List them under Expressions I May Need.

 C. As a class, discuss in English any special or unusual facts or characteristics of your local climate and weather. Record them on Climate and Weather Expressions Worksheet 8.W. File your worksheet in your portfolio for later use.

D. Now think about the ways in which weather affects your daily life. In a small group, brainstorm in French the kinds of clothing you wear and the activities you do in different types of weather. Share your ideas with the class, and add to your list any new information you get from your classmates.

Saviez-vous que ...?

France is often referred to as **l'hexagone** (*the hexagon*) because of its geographical shape: Three sides border on water, and three sides border on land. Despite the fact that France is only 80 percent the size of Texas (212,918 square miles, or 567,026 square kilometers), it has several very different regional climates, influenced by its varied geographical features. If you were in France in the winter, for example, you could be skiing in the French Alps, while a friend was enjoying the mild weather of the Mediterranean coast.

 E. Collect a few weather forecasts from your local newspaper and store them in your portfolio for later use.

Explorons le Web!

You can find information about the weather in the U.S. and the world via the World Wide Web. A great variety of information is available on-line—maps showing entire countries and regions, three- to five-day forecasts, and details that are only a few hours old and are updated as often as every three to six hours. Using your preferred search engine, locate several forecasts for your local area on the Web.

Keywords

news
weather
"weather [+ name of area researching]"

Examinez de vraies cartes météo

Weather reports can range from simple statements of the temperature and local conditions to elaborate forecasts that give the long-term outlook and show weather patterns around the country or even around the world. As you prepare to give your weather broadcast, gather some ideas from weather reports you watch on TV and read in the newspaper.

Ressources utiles

- Televised weather report
- VCR
- What's in a Weather Report? Worksheet 8.A.1
- Weather maps from newspapers or the World Wide Web
- Weather Symbols Worksheet 8.A.2

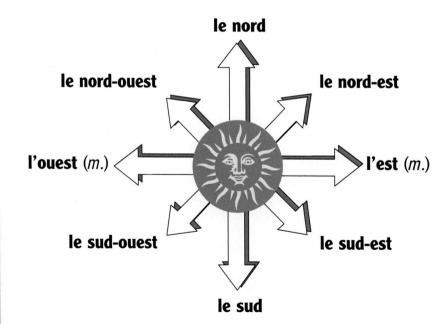

le nord

le nord-ouest   **le nord-est**

l'ouest (*m.*)   **l'est** (*m.*)

le sud-ouest   **le sud-est**

le sud

Connexions

- ☑ Art
- ☑ Géographie
- ☑ Médias
- ☑ Sciences
- ☑ Technologie

1re Étape   Les prévisions de votre région

A. What kinds of information are given in a weather report? Watch one or two on television. If possible, tape one so you can look at it a few times as you collect ideas. Fill out Part 1 of What's in a Weather Report? Worksheet 8.A.1.

B. In your small group, compare in English what you recorded on your worksheets. Then talk about which features of the weather reports you might like to include in your own broadcast. Fill out Part 2 of the worksheet together. Don't worry about details at this point; just gather some ideas that you can develop in the next part of the project.

2e Étape   Comment dit-on en français?

A. In your small group, choose two or three different weather maps that members have collected. As you look at each one, see how much you can say about the weather in French. Use the vocabulary and expressions you've gathered on Worksheets 8.W and 8.A.1 for help. If you use any French expressions that aren't already listed, jot them down. If there's an expression you don't know but want to use, look it up in the list of weather expressions in the Almanac or in a dictionary, and add it to your list.

B. As a class, discuss which expressions are proving most helpful. Be sure to add any new information to Worksheet 8.A.1.

Saviez-vous que ...?

In newspapers published in France, the weather forecast often includes a map. It shows metropolitan France, the land in Europe that you probably think of as France. But at least one more land area is also shown—the island of Corsica (**la Corse**), which is part of France. It's off the southern coast of France in the Mediterranean Sea. In addition, you may see the former French colonies of Morocco (**le Maroc**), Algeria (**l'Algérie**), and Tunisia (**la Tunisie**) on such a map. These French-speaking North African countries are shown because a hot, dry, violent wind (**l'autan**) sometimes blows from North Africa across the Mediterranean into southern and southeastern France.

3ᵉ Étape   Les symboles météorologiques

Weather reports in newspapers and on television generally use symbols such as these below to provide a quick visual overview of the weather. In your small group, look again at the weather maps you've collected, and gather some ideas for weather symbols you might want to use in your weather report. Add them in Column 1 of Weather Symbols Worksheet 8.A.2. Do you have other ideas for weather symbols? Draw them as well. In Column 2, write in French what each symbol stands for. Consult your dictionary or the weather expressions in the Almanac for help. When you're done, add your worksheets to your portfolio.

Explorons le Web!

The Web site of the National Weather Service provides a good deal of information about U.S. weather in the past, present, or future. It also provides definitions of weather symbols. Follow the path: "national weather service," weather maps, chart reference guide.

Formez vos prévisions!

Now that you've gathered some general ideas and information for your weather report, it's time for the details.

Ressources utiles

- Weather Report Decision Worksheet 8.B
- Newspaper weather reports from different times of the year
- Almanacs with information about average annual temperatures

---

1re Étape   Que dit-on pour commencer?

How do you want to begin your weather report in French? With your small group, look at the ideas you recorded on What's in a Weather Report? Worksheet 8.A.1 as well as the possibilities given below. Write a short introduction to your weather report on Weather Report Decision Worksheet 8.B. Have the news anchor introduce the forecaster. Then have the forecaster say "hello" and state the place, the day, and the date.

▶ Voici notre présentatrice météo Hélène Durand.
Bonsoir, mesdames et messieurs.
Voici les prévisions pour Cheyenne, Wyoming.
Demain, c'est le 25 mai.

2e Étape   Quel temps fait-il aujourd'hui?

Connexions

- ✔ Géographie
- ✔ Mathématiques
- ✔ Sciences
- ✔ Technologie

With your small group, choose the day of the year when your weather report will be broadcast. What's the local weather usually like at that time of year? If possible, check a newspaper weather report for the time of year you've chosen, or use an almanac to find information about average temperatures. Then decide what the weather will be like on the day of your broadcast. On Worksheet 8.B, write in French: the date you've chosen, the high and low temperatures in degrees Fahrenheit, and at least five weather expressions in French to describe the local weather for the day you've chosen.

3ᵉ Étape Comment mesurer la température?

 As you may know, most U.S. weather maps use the Fahrenheit scale to report temperatures. Your French-speaking viewers will understand your weather report better if you give the temperatures in degrees Celsius (C). Use the thermometer and the Fahrenheit and Celsius conversion chart in the weather section of the Almanac to learn how to change temperatures from one scale to another. Convert the temperatures you provided in the **2ᵉ Étape** from Fahrenheit to Celsius. Check your results with your group and record them on Weather Report Decision Worksheet 8.B. From now on, give all your temperatures in Celsius!

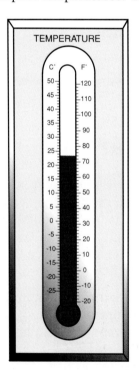

4ᵉ Étape Le temps des jours prochains

 A. What's the weather outlook for the next day? Your group's forecast should include some change in the weather. Write your ideas on Weather Report Decision Worksheet 8.B, and include at least five weather expressions.

B. An extended weather forecast (**les prévisions météorologiques**) usually outlines the weather and temperatures for the next three to seven days. On Weather Report Decision Worksheet 8.B write a short statement in French describing the general weather trends for the next three days.

Un peu plus

Find out the times of sunrise and sunset for the time of year you're covering in your weather report. If you live near a coast, include the times of the high and low tides as well.

Vocabulaire

Il fait [du brouillard].	*It's [foggy/misty/hazy].*
Il y a possibilité de [neige dans les Alpes].	*There's a chance of [snow in the Alps].*
La température minimum/ maximum va être de [20° C].	*The low/high temperature will be [20° C].*
La température minimum/ maximum a été de [20° C].	*The low/high temperature was [20° C].*
Le soleil va se lever à [7 h 20].	*Sunrise is at [7:20 A.M.].*
Le soleil va se coucher à [19 h 37].	*Sunset is at [7:37 P.M.].*
La marée haute/basse est à [6 h 24].	*High/low tide is at [6:24 A.M.].*

Saviez-vous que ... ?

Many languages use colorful expressions to talk about the weather. You've heard the English expression *It's raining cats and dogs.* When there's a downpour in France, they say *It's raining ropes* (**Il pleut des cordes**). But French speakers also use animal images to describe the weather. When it's very cold, for example, **Il fait un froid de loup** (*It's wolf cold*) or **Il fait un froid de canard** (*It's duck cold*). If the weather's lousy, you can say **Il fait un temps de chien** (*It's dog weather*). And when a fierce wind is blowing, you might hear a French speaker say, **Il fait un vent à décorner les bœufs** (*The wind could blow the horns off a steer*). Try using some of these expressions in your weather report!

Illustrez la météo

From simple illustrations to advanced radar maps and satellite pictures, visual aids are an important part of a television weather report. They can help us to understand weather patterns or give us a quick overview of the most important weather information. A weather forecaster (**le présentateur/la présentatrice météo**) can also use maps and pictures as visual cues for guidance during the weather report.

Ressources utiles

- What's in a Weather Report? Worksheet 8.A.1
- Weather Symbols Worksheet 8.A.2
- Weather Report Decision Worksheet 8.B
- Poster board or foam core
- Colored markers, removable tape, index cards

1re Étape   Vos idées

How can you illustrate the weather in your televised weather report? Before you look at the ideas in the following steps, review the ones you collected on What's in a Weather Report? Worksheet 8.A.1. In your small group, choose an idea you think would work well and discuss what you need to do to carry it out. Make a list of any materials you need, and divide the work among the members of your group.

2e Étape   La carte météo

Connexions

- ☑ Art
- ☑ Géographie
- ☑ Sciences
- ☑ Stratégies d'étude

A weather map (**la carte météo**) is a basic part of most televised weather reports. Your group is going to create one with removable weather symbols, so you can show changes in the weather over a period of time. If you're giving your weather report live, you'll need to create a map large enough to be seen easily by your audience. If you're videotaping your broadcast, you can feature close-ups of a smaller map.

A. With your small group, locate a map of your state or region to use as a model for your weather map. On poster board, foam core, or another sturdy material, draw the basic outline of your forecast area. Add your town and a few other important towns and landmarks.

B. Now make some symbols to illustrate the weather you've described on Worksheet 8.B. Look at Worksheet 8.A.2 for ideas about how to represent the weather. On poster board, draw the symbols you need, color them, and cut them out. Attach them to your map with removable tape.

C. Finally, create removable labels that you can attach to the map to show each temperature and day of the week you're illustrating. On blank index cards or pieces of poster board, write each temperature in degrees Celsius and each day of the forecast in French. Attach the labels with removable tape when they're needed.

3ᵉ Étape   Illustrez votre prévision météo

Now give an illustrated long-term forecast. On a piece of poster board, draw a row of pictures illustrating the general weather conditions for each day of the long-term forecast you outlined on Weather Report Decision Worksheet 8.B. Include the high and low temperatures as well.

Saviez-vous que ... ?

In the U.S., the severe arctic winds and snow that come out of Canada into the Northeast are often called "the Montreal Express." In France, **le mistral** is a fierce cold wind from the north that blows down the Rhone River valley to the Mediterranean. It reaches speeds of 200 km/h. The branch of the high-speed train (**le TGV—le train à grande vitesse**) that runs between Paris and Marseilles is named **le mistral** after this wind.

Le bulletin spécial

W eather reports sometimes go beyond merely describing the local and regional weather. When there are important weather-related events, on-the-scene reports help viewers understand the true impact of the weather. Visitors to your area will appreciate hearing about local events and activities affected by the weather.

Ressources utiles

■ What's in a Weather Report? Worksheet 8.A.1
■ Props for staging a live report

1re Étape   ## Qu'est-ce qui nous attend?

With your small group, decide what kind of weather you want to show in your on-the-scene report: a snowstorm? a very cold or windy day? a heat wave? a thunderstorm or hurricane? Brainstorm ideas for staging your weather scene. For example, a fan can be used to create the effect of a strong wind; a shivering reporter dressed in a heavy parka can show how cold it is; or lights turned on and off can depict lightning. Use your imagination!

2e Étape   ## Une émission sur place

Write a short script in French for your on-the-scene reporter. Describe the weather and what it feels like to be there. Include some interviews with passersby as well. What do they think about the weather — rain for five straight days or three feet of snow? How do they feel? How do they stay warm or keep cool? How are they dressed? What are they planning to do in this weather?

Connexions

☑ Art
☑ Sciences
☑ Technologie

Vocabulaire

Que pensez-vous du temps aujoud'hui?	*What do you think of the weather today?*
Ça m'agace.	*It's getting on my nerves.*
Qu'il fait beau!	*It's beautiful out!*
C'est difficile à supporter.	*It's hard to put up with.*
On doit supporter ___.	*You have to put up with ___.*

3e Étape Autre chose?

 Look at the features you listed in Part 1 of Worksheet 8.A.1. Think of other features you'd like to add to your weather report. With your group, draw up a plan and divide up the work.

Un peu plus

Create a commercial for a weather-related product (umbrellas, ski resorts, air conditioners, and so on) to be broadcast during your weather report.

Saviez-vous que ...?

In France, the headquarters for information on current French weather and weather research is located in Toulouse. This center is connected to weather stations in French-speaking countries and regions worldwide. It also interacts with weather research centers in other nations throughout the world. One such station is located in the Caribbean and can help the U.S. Weather Bureau detect and track hurricanes that may hit the U.S.

Présentez vos prévisions!

It's almost airtime. How are all the parts of your weather broadcast going to fit together? It's time to put the final touches on your work.

Ressources utiles

- All materials created for the weather report
- Equipment to videotape the weather report

1re Étape   Organisez-vous!

With your group, make the following important decisions. Be sure to record them.

1. In what order are you going to present the different parts of your weather report? Make an outline, leaving a couple of lines free between items for additional notes.

2. Which group member will present each part of the weather report and special features? Record this information on your outline, and make sure that each person has a script for his or her part.

3. Are you going to give your weather report live or record it on videotape? If you videotape it, decide who will record each part. Add this information to your outline.

4. How are you going to change scenes and set up and use maps and other props? Videotaping will give you more flexibility in your performance, since you can record your report in parts and stop the camera at any point to set up a new scene. If you're performing live, make sure you know who's responsible for setting up materials and helping the presenters in each part of your report. Add this information to your outline.

Connexions

- ☑ Médias
- ☑ Stratégies d'étude

2ᵉ Étape   Préparez vos commentaires!

The key to a good performance is practice. Rehearse individually and as a group, using your maps, pictures, and other props. Have someone in your group coach you as you practice. Remember that your visual aids can help guide you through your weather report. Simply pointing to different symbols can remind you of what you want to say.

3ᵉ Étape   Vous êtes météorologistes!

Now it's time for the evening news and the weather report! Flip the channels and compare weather forecasts!

4ᵉ Étape   Fait-il beau ou mauvais?

So which forecast is accurate? You decide! You'll find out tomorrow!

Saviez-vous que ...?

Weather-related records can be hard to believe. Forecasters sometimes quote them to help people understand how local weather events compare to those in other places. Here are some records from the French-speaking world. The island of Réunion (off the coast of Africa) holds three world records for the greatest amount of rainfall:

- 45 inches (114 centimeters) in 12 hours
- 72 inches (182.5 centimeters) in 24 hours
- 156 inches (395 centimeters) in 5 days

In France, the town of Bessans holds the world record for the most snow in 19 hours: 68 inches (173 centimeters).

La bonne santé

In this project your class will set up and run a health center. Its purpose will be to help educate French-speaking clients about the benefits of a healthy lifestyle and how to maintain their health through nutrition, exercise, and so on. Working with a group of your classmates, you'll accomplish the following tasks along the way:

- Complete and label a drawing of the human body
- Research good nutrition and make a food pyramid
- Create a chart illustrating the health benefits of physical activity
- Design forms to be used by clients and health counselors
- Create a brochure to advertise your health center
- Set up and run your health center

À votre santé!

Connexions

In the process of opening a health center, you'll sharpen your skills in many areas.

☑ Art   ☐ Musique
☐ Géographie   ☑ Santé et nutrition
☐ Histoire   ☑ Sciences
☐ Mathématiques   ☑ Stratégies d'étude
☐ Médias   ☑ Technologie

Look for the **Connexions** boxes throughout this project.

Warm-up: Qu'est-ce que la santé?

Ressources utiles

- Newspapers and magazines
- Cardboard, poster board, or construction paper
- Tape, string, or stapler

1re Étape   Les photos

Working in your group, search magazines and newspapers to find pictures that you associate with good health. They might include pictures of athletes, people exercising, or healthy foods, to give you just a few ideas. Gather a variety of images.

2e Étape   Un collage

A. With your group, arrange the pictures you've found into a colorful collage showing many different images of health. Label as many of the pictures as possible with words and descriptive captions in French.

B. Look at some of the other collages in your class to see how many different ideas, activities, and topics are associated with the word *health*. Then, have a short class discussion about what you've discovered.

3e Étape   Un dossier sur la santé

At the end of each section in this unit, you'll need to save what you've made and learned for use later in your health center. To organize this material, your group needs to make a large portfolio. (It should be about 2 feet x 3 feet when closed.) You can do this by tying, taping, or stapling together two large pieces of cardboard, poster board, or construction paper. Attaching a handle will make your portfolio easier to carry. Label your folder **Dossier sur la santé** (*health resources folder*).

Saviez-vous que...?

Many French expressions use the word **sucre** (*sugar*) in terms of affection, such as **mon petit trésor en sucre** (literally, *my little sugary treasure*). **Sucre** may also describe the way someone looks at life—**être tout sucre tout miel** (*to be all sugar, all honey*). In English, this expression means *to be all sweetness and light*. Another expression, **cet enfant n'est pas fait en sucre quand même** (*that child isn't really made of sugar*) has two English equivalents: *For goodness sake, the child won't break*, or *The child won't melt*.

 # Le corps humain

An important resource in a health facility is an illustration of the human body. It's used to illustrate the bones, muscles, and systems of the body, such as how blood flows through the body or how food is digested.

Ressources utiles

- French-English dictionary
- Encyclopedia or anatomy book
- Colored markers
- Human Body Worksheet 9.A
- Health resources folder

 1ʳᵉ Étape ## Les parties du corps

On Human Body Worksheet 9.A, give French names for the parts of the body that can be seen by looking at a person, such as nose, ears, arms, and toes. Before you consult your textbook or a dictionary, see how many you can come up with on your own!

 2ᵉ Étape ## L'intérieur du corps

A. With your group, find an illustration of the human body's internal organs, such as the heart, lungs, and stomach, in an encyclopedia or anatomy book. Make a list of eight major internal organs to add to the illustration on Human Body Worksheet 9.A. Then find their French names and write them down as well.

 B. Draw the basic forms of eight internal organs on the illustration on Human Body Worksheet 9.A. Refer to the illustration in the encyclopedia or anatomy book to be sure you locate them properly in the body. Finally, use colored markers to label the organs.

Connexions

- ☑ Sciences
- ☑ Stratégies d'étude

3e Étape   **Le dossier sur la santé**

Add completed Human Body Worksheet 9.A to your health resources folder for later use.

Saviez-vous que...?

In France, people like to stay in shape (**en forme**). As a result, about one French person in five regularly participates in a sport. Rather than push themselves to the limit or make good looks their goal, most people simply try to stay in shape and improve their skills. Except for soccer, the French have traditionally been more interested in individual rather than in team sports. Walking and hiking (**la marche** and **la randonnée**) are also very popular forms of exercise.

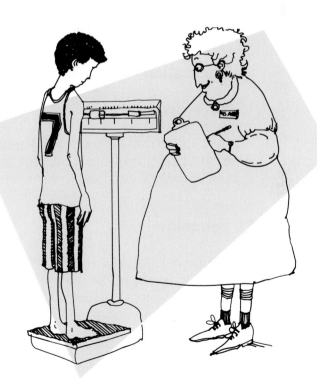

La nutrition

Proper eating habits are necessary for a healthy lifestyle. One function of a health center is educating clients about good nutrition. You may be surprised by how much you already know about eating sensibly!

Ressources utiles

- ■ Encyclopedia, health or science textbooks, and books about health and nutrition
- ■ French-English dictionary
- ■ Colored markers or computer-drawing software, poster board, paper
- ■ Nutrition Worksheet 9.B
- ■ Health resources folder

1re Étape   ## L'alimentation

In your group, brainstorm in French a list of as many different foods as you can without using a dictionary. Refer to the food vocabulary in the Almanac to get started. You may be surprised at how much you know! When your list is ready, share it with another group in your class, and expand your list with ideas from the other group.

2e Étape   ## La pyramide

A. Nutritionists, people who study how the body uses different foods, have developed the food pyramid as a guide for sensible eating. It shows what people should eat to get the right amount of each food group. Look at the food pyramid in the Warm-up section. Write the different types of foods in French on the pyramid in Part 1 of Nutrition Worksheet 9.B. Now record the foods you listed in the **1re Étape** in the correct section of the food pyramid. Where would you list **les haricots verts,** for example? Or what about **le yaourt**?

Connexions

- ☑ Art
- ☑ Santé et nutrition
- ☑ Sciences
- ☑ Technologie

B. What is good nutrition? In your group, discuss in English what you know about the food pyramid and good nutrition. Then use colored markers or a computer with drawing software to draw a large food pyramid on poster board or a large piece of paper. Label each part of the pyramid with the French name for the type of food that belongs there. Using the list your group created in the **1ʳᵉ Étape**, draw foods in each category on your pyramid and label them in French. Display your food pyramid in the health center.

3ᵉ Étape — Les règles

The bottom level of the food pyramid is the largest, showing that such foods should be eaten the most. The foods on the top level should be eaten in the smallest quantities. Using your food pyramid, create a list of four rules for healthy eating. Record your rules for proper nutrition in Part 2 of Nutrition Worksheet 9.B. Add your food pyramid and Nutrition Worksheet 9.B to your health resources folder.

Vocabulaire

On doit [+ *infinitive*].   *You should ___.*
Il faut [+ *infinitive*].   *You must ___.*
Il est conseillé   *It is suggested/advised that*
de/d' [+ *verb*].   *you ___.*
Vous devez manger/boire ___.   *You should eat/drink ___.*

Saviez-vous que...?

In French, there are many colorful figures of speech that refer to the human body. For example, you would say **"Ça m'a coupé les jambes"** (*It cut off my legs*) if you were so shocked by something that you couldn't move. **Avoir l'estomac dans les talons** (*to have your stomach in your heels*) is to be very hungry. **Coûter les yeux de la tête** (*to cost the eyes of the head*) is to be extremely expensive, or to cost an arm and a leg.

L'activité physique

hysical activity and exercise are necessary for overall well-being. Your health center will give visitors information about how proper exercise can improve their health.

Ressources utiles

■ Encyclopedia and books about health

■ Exercise Worksheet 9.C

■ Nutrition Worksheet 9.B

■ Health resources folder

1re Étape   L'exercice

A. There are many different ways to get exercise. On your own, list in French five of your favorite free-time activities **(les loisirs)** that use physical energy. Write them under **Loisirs favoris** in Part 1, column 1, on Exercise Worksheet 9.C. For ideas, refer to the list of sports in the Almanac.

▶ **faire une promenade à bicyclette** (*to go bike riding*)

B. Continue on your own on the same worksheet. In Part 2, column 1, under **Activités quotidiennes** (*Everyday activities*), write the names of three everyday activities or chores that you think take enough energy to offer health benefits.

▶ **tondre le gazon** (*mowing the lawn*)

Connexions

☑ Santé et nutrition
☑ Sciences
☑ Stratégies d'étude

2e Étape   Les bénéfices de l'exercice

A. What are the health benefits of all eight activities you've listed? Decide which part(s) of the body are exercised during each activity. Record them on Exercise Worksheet 9.C in column 2 under **Parties du corps.**

▶ faire une promenade à bicyclette   le cœur
   tondre le gazon   les jambes

B. In your group, use the phrases below to compare your lists of exercises, activities, and health benefits. Come up with a list of four suggestions for getting exercise, and write them in Part 3 of Exercise Worksheet 9.C for use in your health center.

Vocabulaire

J'aime [+ *infinitive*].   *I like to ___.*
C'est bon pour [une partie du corps].   *It's good for ___.*

Un peu plus

Use some of the materials listed in the **Ressources utiles** box to find out how many calories are burned during each activity you've listed. Remember to include how long you must perform the activity to use that number of calories. Add this information to Exercise Worksheet 9.C in column 3, under **Nombre de calories en combien de temps**. Add the worksheet to your health resources folder.

Les formulaires

Your health center will communicate with clients in various ways. You'll talk on the phone with them, interview them in person, and educate them with the charts and pictures you've made. But first you'll need to get some basic information from your clients by using a standard form that they will fill out when they visit the center. Such information will be used by doctors, nurses, counselors, the billing department, and so on.

Ressources utiles

- Computer with a word-processing program
- French-English dictionary
- Health resources folder

1re Étape Des questions importantes

As a class, brainstorm a list of questions in French that a receptionist at a health center might ask to gather information about clients. Come up with at least five useful questions. Go over the questions to make sure you haven't forgotten anything important. Write the questions on the board.

2e Étape Créer les formulaires

In your group, organize the information you brainstormed into a French-language form. You might want to design it on the computer. Be sure to include blanks for the visitors to fill out and a space for the health counselor's comments. Since group members will take turns playing different roles, be sure to make multiple copies. Add the forms to your health resources folder for use in Section F.

Connexions

☑ Santé et nutrition
☑ Technologie

E La brochure

I n order to attract clients, it's important to advertise the services available at your health center. One of the best ways to do this is by making a brochure to distribute to the public.

Ressources utiles

- Computer with a word-processing program
- Health resources folder
- The local telephone book with yellow pages

1re Étape Les détails du centre

A. Working in your small group, come up with a creative idea for a French name for your health center. It may be helpful to review the information in your health resources folder. Consider practical names (**Centre de services médicaux**) and clever ones (**Chaque jour une pomme …**). Present your ideas to your class, and together choose one to be the name of your center. All of the groups will be working together in the center, so you need only one name.

B. As a class, decide, in French, on the schedule of your center. Will it be open only on weekdays? Will it operate any evenings in order to accommodate clients' work schedules? Come up with a list of hours (**les heures d'ouverture**) to include in your brochure. Remember to start with **lundi** as the first day of the week. Since you're making a schedule, use a 24-hour clock—1:00 P.M. is **13 h**, 2:00 P.M. is **14 h**, and so forth.

C. Next, decide what general information about your health center will need to be included in your brochure. Brainstorm this information in English, while your teacher lists it on the board. Remember to include the basic details about your clinic (name, address, and so on) as well as a description of its function, services, and so forth. Will you include any drawings or photos?

Connexions

 Stratégies
   d'étude
 Technologie

CHAQUE JOUR UNE POMME...

997, avenue des Médecins

 67000 Strasbourg

Tél: 03.88.55.43.20

2ᵉ Étape　L'organisation

Divide the information you listed on the board among the small groups in your class. Each group will be responsible for creating one section of the informative brochure about your clinic (for example, A. Our mission, B. Nutrition courses, and so forth). Remember that you may need to invent some of the information, such as the French-language address, phone number, and so on. A word processor may make the brochure look more professional. Use the resources in the **Ressources utiles** box to help you, and be creative!

3ᵉ Étape　Créer la brochure

When all the groups are finished, put your brochure together. Make multiple copies or ask your teacher to photocopy them for you. Put your brochures in your health resources folder.

Un @ peu plus

Design business cards for your health center.

Le centre est ouvert!

Your health center is nearly ready to open. There are just a few final preparations to be made. When everything is ready, open the center.

> **Ressources utiles**
>
> ■ Completed health resources folders, including Worksheets 9.B and 9.C, food pyramids, brochures
> ■ Poster board and colored markers
> ■ French-English dictionary

 1ʳᵉ Étape **Les derniers détails**

A. Choose one group to make a sign in French for the outside of your center. Post the name of the center and the days and hours it's open to the public.

B. Another group in your class should make smaller signs for the different departments of the center such as the reception area, waiting room, and counselors. Make your signs in French, of course!

LA SALLE D'ATTENTE
(waiting room)

LE BUREAU DE RÉCEPTION
(RECEPTION DESK)

Connexions

☑ Art
☑ Santé et nutrition

Les conseillers
(counselors)

c. Meanwhile, the remaining groups should set up the classroom for use as a health center. Chairs need to be placed in the waiting room, desks arranged for the receptionists and health counselors, and so on. Hang the collages and drawings of the human body and food pyramids in appropriate places in the classroom for use in the center. Finally, post the signs that the groups have created and put the brochures on display.

2ᵉ Étape — Prêts?

Within each group, decide who will play the roles of receptionists, health counselors, and clients at the center.

Receptionists (**les réceptionnistes**) need pens and the forms you created. Health counselors (**les conseillers**) should take the remaining health resources from the health resources folders and sit at the desks placed in the counseling area to wait for clients. Clients (**les clients**) should decide on at least two questions to ask the health counselors, along with the reason for their visit to the clinic. Is it to learn about health in general? to learn new exercises? to get nutritional information? Jot this information down in French.

3ᵉ Étape — À votre service!

Your health center is open. Clients enter, talk with receptionists, and fill out forms. A few clients call the center to inquire about hours and receptionists answer.

▶ Bonjour/Bonsoir. Ici [*name of clinic*].

Some receptionists can sit near the door of the classroom, handing out forms. Others answer phones. Still others receive completed forms and show clients in to speak with health counselors.

Health counselors ask clients how they feel and what they want to learn at the center. Using information from the food pyramid and from Nutrition Worksheet 9.B and Exercise Worksheet 9.C, counselors should suggest nutrition and exercise options to clients. After talking with a counselor, clients may then become receptionists or counselors, so that everyone gets to play more than one role. Be creative!

Vocabulaire

les réceptionnistes:

    Je peux vous aider?

    Remplissez ce formulaire, s'il vous plaît.

les clients:

    Qu'est-ce qu'il faut écrire ici?

    Combien de temps est-ce que je dois attendre un conseiller?

    Est-ce que je dois prendre rendez-vous pour voir un conseiller?

    Je me sens [fatigué(e), mal, stressé(e), etc.].

    Quels exercices sont bons pour [part of body]?

    Quelle alimentation est bonne pour la santé?

    Je voudrais des renseignements sur ___.

les conseillers:

    Que voulez-vous savoir?

    [Les fruits] sont bons pour la santé.

    [La natation] est excellent pour les muscles.

receptionists:

    May I help you?

    Please fill out this form.

clients:

    What do you need to write here?

    How long do I have to wait to see a counselor?

    Do I have to make an appointment to see a counselor?

    I feel [tired, bad, stressed, etc.].

    Which exercises are good for [part of the body]?

    Which foods are healthy?

    I'd like information about ___.

counselors:

    What do you want to know?

    [Fruit] is good for you.

    [Swimming] is great for the muscles.

Ouvrons un restaurant!

Using your knowledge of the foods and cultures of French-speaking countries and regions, you and your group will open your own restaurant. In the process you will:

- Choose a type of restaurant and a name
- Decide on a location
- Decide on your restaurant's specialties
- Devise a decorating scheme and select background music
- Hire staff
- Design your menu
- Advertise your restaurant
- Prepare a shopping list of the foods you need to make your menu items

On opening day you will set up your restaurant in the classroom, greet customers, seat them, take their orders, and enjoy your food.

Bon appétit!

Connexions

In the process of opening a restaurant, you will sharpen your skills in many areas.

- ✔ Art
- ✔ Géographie
- ✔ Histoire
- ✔ Mathématiques
- ✔ Médias
- ✔ Musique
- ✔ Santé et nutrition
- ☐ Sciences
- ✔ Stratégies d'étude
- ✔ Technologie

Look for the **Connexions** boxes throughout this project.

Warm-up: À table!

Ressources utiles

- Cookbooks and magazines with recipes from French-speaking countries and regions
- Guidebooks for French-speaking countries and regions
- The World Wide Web
- Folder or portfolio to store your research

A. With a small group of your classmates, discuss in French some of your favorite foods. Refer to the food vocabulary in the Almanac.

Vocabulaire

| Qu'est-ce que tu aimes manger? | *What do you like to eat?* |
| Mon plat préféré… | *My favorite dish . . .* |

B. Now think about any experiences you have had with French restaurants in the U.S. Mention foods from French-speaking countries or regions that you have tasted or have heard about. Have you tried them? Would you like to? Are they different from your own favorite foods? Discuss your ideas with your group.

C. Using some of the resources listed in the **Ressources utiles** box, find some information about foods and meals in a French-speaking country or region. Write down in French at least two interesting facts to share with your group. Then put the facts in your folder.

Explorons le Web!

Begin your Web search for information about foods in French-speaking countries by clicking on the Society and Culture or Regional sections of your Web guide. Continue narrowing your search by clicking on the subsections provided, for example Food and Drink or Countries and Cultures. Finally, click on the name of a French-speaking country and then investigate the various suggested Web sites. Bookmark useful sites.

D. In your group, discuss what you have learned about foods and meals in the countries you chose. Did anything surprise you? As a class, discuss any differences and similarities you have discovered between foods and mealtimes in the U.S. and in French-speaking countries and regions.

Un peu plus

As homework or in your group, make a chart showing the usual mealtimes and the typical foods eaten at each meal in the U.S. and in one or more of the French-speaking countries and regions. The U.S. section should be in English, and the French section in French. Use the following table as a guide.

Meal/Repas	U.S.	[French-speaking country]
breakfast/**le petit déjeuner**	time: typical foods:	l'heure: le repas typique:
lunch/**le déjeuner**	time: typical foods:	l'heure: le repas typique:
dinner/**le dîner**	time: typical foods:	l'heure: le repas typique:

Les premières décisions

When opening a restaurant, or any business, you must make many decisions—some big, some small. You are going to begin by choosing the type of restaurant you will open and deciding on a name for it.

Ressources utiles

- French–English dictionary
- Business Decisions Worksheet 10.A
- Portfolio or folder for storing worksheets

1re Étape Quel type de restaurant?

Keeping in mind what you have learned about foods and mealtimes in French-speaking countries and regions, decide with your group what type of restaurant you would like to open. Are you interested in a café-style restaurant with outdoor seating or a fastfood restaurant for business people? a carry-out place at the beach? an after-ski coffee shop? Will your restaurant be casual or elegant? large or small?

2e Étape Nommez votre restaurant

A. Working with your group, brainstorm a list of adjectives in French that could describe your restaurant. Use your dictionary or textbook for further inspiration.

B. Using your list of adjectives and your creativity, work with your group to invent a clever French name for your restaurant.

Connexions

☑ Stratégies d'étude

Mom's   **Le Restaurant des artistes**

Chez Ondine

Pasta Palace

The Greasy Spoon

L'Auberge des cigognes

The Blue Onion

Le Plateau de fromages   *Le pêcheur*

Fred's Roadside Diner

La Côte d'or   Fish n' Fowl

3ᵉ Étape   Quelles décisions?

Now that you have made two key decisions about your restaurant, ask your teacher for a copy of Business Decisions Worksheet 10.A and record these and future decisions. Put the worksheet in your portfolio (or folder) for future reference.

Saviez-vous que ... ?

In France, people of all ages go to cafés. Students go there to eat, debate, or study. Shoppers and business people have lunch in cafés, and tourists relax there as they enjoy the French atmosphere. In good weather, tables extend out onto the sidewalk and customers choose between sitting inside (**à l'intérieur**) or outside (**à la terrasse**). Some cafés offer only simple and inexpensive snacks while others offer full meals. In France, there is something for everyone at a café!

L'endroit idéal

In opening a business, location is everything. Restaurants are often placed in or near well-populated areas to attract as much business as possible. Restaurants need to be easy for their customers to find and there needs to be a demand for them in the chosen location. It may be better, for example, to open a bakery-café near a movie theater rather than near a health club. Locating your restaurant near a busy intersection or a tourist attraction would also help bring in customers. Or perhaps you are a risk-taker and want to locate it in a lesser-known area.

Ressources utiles

- Travel guides; maps of French-speaking countries, regions, and cities
- Encyclopedias, travel magazines, guidebooks
- Business Decisions Worksheet 10.A
- The World Wide Web

Connexions

- ☑ Art
- ☑ Géographie
- ☑ Technologie

1re Étape **Quelles sont les possibilités?**

A. Keeping in mind the type of restaurant you have chosen to establish, discuss the following questions in your group:

1. Quelle est l'importance du site de votre restaurant?

   Vaut-il mieux ouvrir votre restaurant à la campagne ou en ville? au bord de la mer? près d'un fleuve? à la montagne? dans une rue du centre-ville?

   Comment les gens vont-ils venir à votre restaurant? Y-a-t-il des transports en commun près de votre restaurant? Les gens vont-ils conduire au restaurant?

2. Qui est la clientèle de votre restaurant? des touristes? des familles? des hommes/femmes d'affaires?

B. Using the resources listed in the **Ressources utiles** box, look for locations that fit the criteria you have established.

Explorons le Web!

Use the Recreation or Travel section of a Web guide to link to listings of restaurants or Web sites of restaurants in cities in French-speaking countries and regions.

2e Étape **Le choix final**

A. In your group, discuss the possible locations for your restaurant and decide on an ideal location together.

 B. On Business Decisions Worksheet 10.A, write a brief description in French of your restaurant's location, including important geographical markers. Explain why you chose the location. Put the worksheet in your portfolio (or folder) for future reference.

 C. As homework or in your group, draw a map of the location, labeling landmarks, geographical features, and streets (in French, of course!). Mark the exact location of your restaurant.

C Les recettes

Many restaurants have one or two menu items that are their customers' favorites. In locations near the ocean, for example, shellfish may be the specialty. In Switzerland, fondue (a hot dish of melted cheese that is eaten with bread) is often the featured item.

Ressources utiles

- Cookbooks and food magazines
- The World Wide Web

1ʳᵉ Étape ## Les specialités de la maison

Look through cookbooks or food magazines to find recipes for menu items you might want to feature in your restaurant. Put together a recipe book of dishes you want to serve.

Explorons le Web!

You can find recipes on the Web! Use a search engine and the keywords to the right or click on the Lifestyles, Travel, or Culture sections of a Web guide. Then continue narrowing your search by clicking in appropriate sections such as Food and Drink, Recipes, or Restaurants, until you reach a list of Web sites.

Keywords

recette
restaurant
cuisine
"gastronomie + [adj. of nationality]"

Connexions

 ☑ Mathématiques
☑ Santé et nutrition
☑ Stratégies d'étude
 ☑ Technologie

2ᵉ Étape   La recette secrète

Work with your group to choose one item from your recipe book that you would like to feature as your house specialty. Remember to take into account the location of your restaurant.

Saviez-vous que...?

Measurements for ingredients in recipes from French-speaking countries may vary from those of a typical recipe in the U.S. For example, flour is usually measured by weight (in grams) rather than by volume (in cups), and liquids are measured in liters.

Un peu plus

Imagine that your group chose the recipe that follows as your restaurant's specialty. Adapt it to the quantity needed to feed your customers!

Citron pressé

- 12 citrons
- 1.5 litres d'eau
- 300 grammes de sucre

Mettez des glaçons dans un pichet. Ajoutez le jus des citrons. Ajoutez le sucre et l'eau. Goûtez. Corrigez en ajoutant encore de l'eau et du sucre selon votre goût. Servez-le froid. Pour 6 personnes.

A. Keeping in mind the size and the clientele of your restaurant, estimate the number of people per day who will be ordering your house specialty. If your recipe serves more than one person, divide the number of servings into the number of customers per day who will order the item. The result is the number of batches of the recipe you will need to make in one day. For example, the lemonade recipe above serves six. If sixty people per day will order lemonade, then the number of pitchers of lemonade needed is ten.

B. You now need to increase the ingredient amounts in your recipe. To do this, multiply the quantity of each ingredient in your recipe by the number of batches needed. Here are the calculations for the lemonade recipe.

Citron pressé

10 x 12 citrons = 120 citrons

10 x 1.5 litres d'eau = 15 litres d'eau

10 x 300 grammes de sucre = 3000 grammes de sucre

Vocabulaire

multiplié par	*multiplied by*
divisé par	*divided by*
égalent	*equal(s)*

Le décor

The ambiance, or atmosphere, of a restaurant is established subtly through the décor of the dining room, the lighting, and the background music.

Ressources utiles

- Cookbooks and food magazines
- Magazines showing decorating ideas
- Guidebooks for French-speaking countries and regions
- Art books or pictures of artwork from French-speaking countries
- Recordings of popular, traditional, and classical music from French-speaking countries
- Business Decisions Worksheet 10.A
- The World Wide Web and encyclopedias

Vocabulaire

la bougie	*candle*
le carrelage	*tiled floor*
décorer	*to decorate*
l'éclairage (*m.*)	*lighting*
la lumière tamisée/diffuse	*soft lighting*
le papier peint	*wallpaper*
le parquet	*hardwood floor*
peindre	*to paint*
la peinture	*paint (for walls)*
le plancher	*floor*
le tapis	*rug*
tapisser	*to paper*

Connexions
- ☑ Art
- ☑ Histoire
- ☑ Médias
- ☑ Musique
- ☑ Technologie

1re Étape   Les idées générales

A. Keeping in mind the type of restaurant you have chosen, discuss the following questions:

1. Quelles couleurs voulez-vous utiliser dans le restaurant?

2. Que voulez-vous comme plancher? (du parquet? du carrelage?)

3. Comment va être l'éclairage? Allez-vous mettre des bougies sur les tables?

B. Draw a picture of your interior-decorating scheme or cut out and compile magazine photos that reflect your ideas. Label the various elements in French, using the preceding **Vocabulaire** section as a guide.

2e Étape   L'art

A. As homework or in your group, consult textbooks, art books, and encyclopedias to identify four pieces of art to decorate your restaurant.

B. Present one piece of art to your group and explain in French or in English why you have chosen it.

Explorons le Web!

You can also locate information about artists and pictures of their works on the Web. If you already have an artist in mind, use his or her entire name in your Web search. You can enclose the entire name in quotes or first try the last name and then refine your search with the other names. You may, however, want to browse at a museum's Web site for artwork from the country where your restaurant is located. If you find the work of an artist that you like, try a search of that artist's name to find more works.

Keywords

name of artist
name of museum
musée
name of an artistic
  genre (e.g.,
  impressionism)

 **Un peu plus**

Write a brief description in French of each piece of art you have chosen. Include the artist's name, the date of the work, and a brief description of the work.

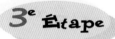 **3ᵉ Étape** **Mettez la table**

Using plastic or paper plates, create the china pattern your restaurant will use. Does your china pattern reflect the cultural heritage of the region where your restaurant is located? For instance, did you use warm and sunny colors for a restaurant featuring Provençal food? nautical themes for a restaurant featuring Breton cuisine? Also choose the color and design of your napkins and place mats or tablecloths.

 **Un peu plus**

Make some sample napkins and place mats.

Saviez-vous que ...?

There's a curious mixture in the foods currently popular in France. People want traditional French foods, but foreign foods also have a large audience. Italian and Chinese cuisine are at the head of the list. But they are followed by ... Mexican! Why? The appeal seems to be spiciness plus the lively décor and music associated with it.

4ᵉ Étape ## La musique

Now it's time to choose some background music to set the right mood.

A. What do you know about the music in the areas associated with the cuisine of your restaurant? Discuss your ideas with your group.

B. There are several ways you can find out more about music from the French-speaking world. Your library may have books and recordings. Using these or other resources, find one or two musicians, music groups, or composers who interest you and share information about them with your group.

C. With your music research in hand, consider the type of restaurant you are going to open. Include its clientele, location, and menu. For instance, a restaurant in downtown Dakar might choose to play traditional African music rather than the latest Top 40 rock hits, unless it caters to students. With your group, choose some background music for your restaurant.

5ᵉ Étape ## Quelles décisions?

Record your decisions about décor and music on Business Decisions Worksheet 10.A and place it in your portfolio (or folder).

Le personnel

No matter how big or small your restaurant is, you need to hire a staff to help you run it.

Ressources utiles

■ Help Wanted ads from French-language newspapers
■ Interview Worksheet 10.E

Vocabulaire

le caissier/la caissière	*cashier*
le chef	*chef*
le cuisinier/la cuisinière	*cook*
le serveur/la serveuse	*waiter/waitress*
le patron/la patronne	*employer, owner*
le/la réceptionniste	*host/hostess*

Connexions

☑ Médias
☑ Technologie

 **Les nécessités**

In your group, discuss the types of positions you need to fill (cooks or chefs, waitstaff, and so forth) in order to run your restaurant. Make a list in French of the help you will need and what their duties will be.

Un @ peu plus

Look at some Help Wanted ads in French-language newspapers, in your textbook, or the ad shown below. Then write an ad for one of the positions open at your new restaurant. Be creative!

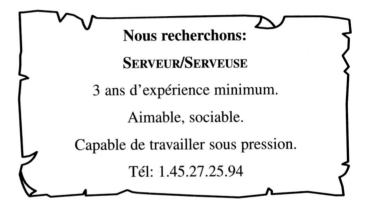

Nous recherchons:

SERVEUR/SERVEUSE

3 ans d'expérience minimum.

Aimable, sociable.

Capable de travailler sous pression.

Tél: 1.45.27.25.94

 **Interviewez les candidats**

Prepare to interview potential employees. Find out each applicant's name, where he or she currently works, and for what position he or she is interviewing. With your group, make a list in French of the questions you can ask to get this information.

 **Les entretiens**

 Take turns interviewing applicants from another group in your class. Record your interview notes on Interview Worksheet 10.E. Put the worksheet in your porfolio (or folder) for future reference.

F Le menu

Choosing dishes and creating the menu is an exciting and challenging aspect of opening a restaurant. Let your taste buds and sense of design run wild!

Ressources utiles

- Cookbooks, food magazines
- Restaurant menus
- Currency exchange rate table from newspaper, bank, or the World Wide Web (see Almanac)
- Computer with drawing tool software
- Colored markers or pencils, paper

Vocabulaire

croustillant(e)	*crisp*
à la vapeur	*steamed*
au four	*baked*
doux/douce	*mild*
épicé(e)	*spicy*
frais/fraîche	*fresh*
frit(e)	*fried*
juteux/juteuse	*juicy*
piquant(e)	*well seasoned*
rôti(e)	*roasted*
sauté(e)	*sautéed*
savoureux/savoureuse	*tasty*

Connexions

- Art
- Mathématiques
- Santé et nutrition
- Technologie

1re Étape   Que voulez-vous servir?

In your group, use some of the resources listed in the **Ressources utiles** box on page 189 and your recipe book from Section C for help in selecting at least two dishes for each category on your menu. Refer to the categories on the following menu as guides, and keep in mind the type of restaurant and location you have chosen.

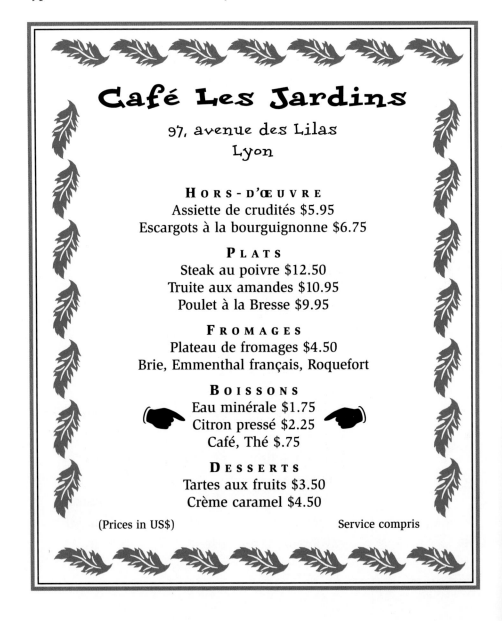

Café Les Jardins

97, avenue des Lilas
Lyon

HORS-D'ŒUVRE
Assiette de crudités $5.95
Escargots à la bourguignonne $6.75

PLATS
Steak au poivre $12.50
Truite aux amandes $10.95
Poulet à la Bresse $9.95

FROMAGES
Plateau de fromages $4.50
Brie, Emmenthal français, Roquefort

BOISSONS
Eau minérale $1.75
Citron pressé $2.25
Café, Thé $.75

DESSERTS
Tartes aux fruits $3.50
Crème caramel $4.50

(Prices in US$)   Service compris

2ᵉ Étape — Les prix

To appeal to tourists or business people from the U.S., you may want to give prices in both U.S. dollars and in the local currency (for example, French **francs** in France or Canadian dollars in Quebec).

A. Consider how much you want to charge for your food and beverages, and assign prices in dollars to your menu items.

B. Now determine the currency of the country where your restaurant is located by consulting the monetary unit chart in the Almanac section of this book. Look up the current rate of exchange for this currency in a local or national newspaper, or use the Web search guidelines supplied in the Almanac below the monetary unit chart.

C. Finally, multiply the dollar price of each of your menu items by the current exchange rate and list your menu prices in the local currency. For example, if a dollar is worth 5 1/2 francs, a $2.00 glass of juice would cost 11 francs.

3ᵉ Étape — Préparez le menu

A. How do you want your menu to look? Before you design your own menu, look at some sample menus for layout and design ideas. Bring in a menu to discuss with your group and compare it to the ones brought in by your classmates. Describe what you like and don't like about the menus.

B. Make a menu using paper, pencils, and markers or design it on the computer, possibly with the aid of drawing tool software. Remember to include the various categories (first course, main course, and so on), the items within those categories, and prices both in the appropriate local currency and in U.S. dollars.

Un peu plus

Expand the menu by including a brief description of each item on it.

4ᵉ Étape   Que désirez-vous manger?

Make a form that the waitstaff can use to take customers' orders. You may wish to use a simplified version of your menu, leaving space next to each item to check off customer orders. Be sure to leave some room at the bottom for the servers to total the bill.

Saviez-vous que...?

When customers order the main dish **(le plat principal)** in a French restaurant, it is generally understood that potatoes or rice and the vegetable of the day come with it. Unless you are in an expensive restaurant, there isn't a choice of vegetables. The French do not automatically expect salad with a meal. If the main dish includes vegetables, then salad is usually not included. On a menu, raw vegetables **(crudités)** are listed under the appetizers. If a salad is eaten, it consists only of lettuce and is served after the main course. A menu often includes two main ways to order—**à la carte** or **à prix fixe. À la carte** means that a customer pays a separate price for each item. The **prix fixe** (*fixed price*) menu is often reasonably priced, but there are fewer choices for the client.

Faisons de la publicité

One of the ways to get customers to come to your restaurant is through advertising. Printed advertisements range from flyers distributed on car windshields to newspaper and magazine ads. Radio and television ads are generally more expensive and complicated than print ads.

Ressources utiles

■ Local newspaper, radio, and television advertisements

■ Advertisements in French from newspapers or magazines

■ Cassette recorder and/or video camera

Vocabulaire

Lumière! Caméra! Action!	*Lights! Camera! Action!*
l'annonce (*f.*)	*advertisement*
au coin du/de la/de l'/des	*at the corner of*
l'acteur/l'actrice	*actor, actress*
la bande sonore	*soundtrack*
couper	*to cut*
les effets de son (*m. pl.*)	*sound effects*
en face du/de la/de l'/des	*across from, facing*
enregistrer	*to videotape*
enregistrer [*something*] sur bande	*to audiotape [something]*
l'inauguration (*f.*)	*grand opening*
le logo	*motto*
le metteur en scène	*director*
la promotion	*special offer*
le prospectus	*flyer*
situé(e)	*located*
tourner	*to shoot*

Connexions

 Art

 Médias

 Musique

☑ Technologie

Ouverture le 3 septembre!

Café Les Jardins

97, avenue des Lilas
Lyon

Nous servons... viandes, poissons, plats végétariens
et une grande variété de spécialités.

Situé au coin de la rue des Jardins et l'avenue des Lilas

1ʳᵉ Étape   Un prospectus

Create a flyer in French announcing the opening of your restaurant.
Include the name, location, and type of food served. Add directions to
the restaurant, including a simple map.

2ᵉ Étape   Une annonce dans les journaux

A. Read some restaurant ads from your local newspaper or Yellow
Pages and from one of the French-language sources listed in the
Ressources utiles box. Choose one ad to discuss with your group,
answering the following questions:

1. Quelle information y a-t-il dans les annonces?

2. Quel est le ton des annonces?

3. Quels mots descriptifs y a-t-il dans les annonces?

4. Y a-t-il de l'art dans les annonces?

B. Now write a brief, catchy newspaper advertisement in French for
your restaurant, using the ads you have analyzed as guides.

Un peu plus

Soyez metteur en scène! Live announcements need to be simple and concise, but also lively and, in the case of television, visually interesting.

A. Choose a favorite radio or television advertisement and describe it in French for your group, answering the following questions:

1. Quelle information est presentée dans l'annonce?

2. Quel est le ton de l'annonce? calme? animé? romantique?

3. Y a-t-il de la musique dans l'annonce? Quels autres sons (*sounds*) entends-tu?

4. Que vois-tu dans l'annonce?

5. Combien de personnes entends-tu ou vois-tu?

B. Write a script in French for your own radio or television ad publicizing your restaurant. Add background sounds and music. Consider interviewing restaurant patrons or staff members. Write! Produce! Direct! Star! If you can, record your radio ad on audiotape, or videotape your television spot.

Au marché

Before your restaurant's grand opening, you will need to order the food required to prepare your dishes.

Ressources utiles

- ■ Menu for your restaurant

1re Étape   Organisez-vous!

Looking carefully at the menu for your restaurant, list in French the categories of foods you need to buy to prepare each menu item (fruits, vegetables, meats, and so on).

2e Étape   La liste des commissions

What fresh food items will you purchase? List each item under the appropriate category, such as fruits, vegetables, and meats.

Fruits	Légumes	Viande
les pêches	les haricots	le steak
les abricots	les tomates	le porc

3e Étape   Les marchands

Finally, next to or above each category on your list, write the type of store in which you will purchase the items. The food stores vocabulary in the Almanac will help you. In many French-speaking countries, people shop at smaller specialty shops, which often have fresher food or a better selection than supermarkets.

Connexions

 Santé et nutrition

Un peu plus

Livraison à domicile. Sometimes restaurant owners order their groceries to be delivered, instead of going to the stores themselves.

A. From your shopping list, choose two stores you need to visit.

B. Working with a partner, take turns calling the shops you chose and ordering in French the groceries you need. Remember to be specific about what you are ordering and to include quantities. (Consult the Almanac section of this book for information on weights and measures.) Give your name, address, and phone number, and discuss prices. Be prepared to present your conversation to the class.

Un peu plus

As homework on the day before the grand opening of your restaurant, get together with your group and prepare the house specialty you will serve to your class the next day. Be ready to explain how the dish is prepared and served.

Le grand jour!

fter all your preparations, the big day is here. You are ready to open your restaurant. **Félicitations!**

Ressources utiles

- Your folder of materials created or gathered so far
- Tableware

Vocabulaire

Qu'est-ce qui est sur le menu?	*What's on the menu?*
Que désirez-vous manger?	*What would you like to eat?*
Et comme boisson?	*And to drink?*
L'addition, s'il vous plaît!	*The bill, please!*
Je vous conseille ___.	*I'd suggest ___.*
Bienvenue(s) à (au) ___.	*Welcome to ___.*
commander	*to order*
la section (non) fumeur	*(non)smoking section*
la spécialité de la maison	*specialty of the house*
le pourboire	*tip*

1re Étape   Les acteurs

Working with your group and the group you interviewed for restaurant positions, choose roles to play in your restaurant. Remember to have some people play the role of customers!

2ᵉ Étape   Mettez les tables

Set up a dining table for your group (push desks together if your classroom does not have tables). Decorate your part of the classroom with any materials you have created or collected. When it is time to open for business, turn on the background music.

3ᵉ Étape   Ouvrez les portes!

Finally, the dining room is ready. The hosts and hostesses greet the customers, who come in chatting in French. The customers are seated, and begin to discuss the menu. Servers come to the table to take orders and answer questions. The rest is up to you!

Saviez-vous que...?

You will usually find **Service compris** or **Service non compris** written on French menus. **Service compris** means that when you get your bill (**l'addition**), the server's tip is included in the total price. **Service non compris** means that the tip is not included, and you must add it.

Almanac

Table of Contents

Web Search Guide

Searching the World Wide Web

The **World Wide Web**[1] contains vast resources that would be hard to locate without **search tools** such as **search engines** and **Web guides.** These two tools allow you to search the Web for useful information by using **keywords** and phrases. You may have already done such searches in English. However, you will find that doing a search in French is most productive if you use French search engines, Web guides, and keywords.

Some of these words and phrases are provided in **Explorons le Web!** boxes in individual projects, but you may need to find others more closely related to your specific topic. Brainstorm helpful French keywords and phrases with other students before you begin your search. When you don't know a word or phrase in French, look in a dictionary or ask your teacher.

Begin your search by **clicking** on the **search button** in your **browser's toolbar.** This will open a **Web site** that offers you a variety of search tools. One of these will probably be automatically chosen for you, but you can change the choice by clicking on the names of other search engines or Web guides. Usually, if you scroll to the bottom of the page, you'll find a pop-up box or **links** that bring you to browsers in other languages. Choose French and click on the link or the **go button**. If the search tool you are using doesn't seem to have an option for French, scroll back up the page and try clicking on a different search tool.

Once you have found a French search tool, it's time to begin your search in earnest. There are two ways that you can do this. The first is to use a Web guide. Web guides select sites for you and list information in general categories with more specific subcategories. Using a Web guide is often the quickest and easiest way to conduct a search. Let's say you want to find descriptions of schools in several French-speaking countries. Try clicking on "travel," then "destinations," then a continent where French is spoken, then a country, then a city. If you are sent to a city's Web site, you will probably find a listing of schools or a way to search for them. Since each Web guide organizes its data differently, **paths** to the same information may vary.

The second way of searching the Web, using either a Web guide or a search engine, is to enter a **search term** in a **text field** and then click on a word like "go," "begin," or "search." This kind of search is useful only when your search term is very specific. If you search for the keyword "school," for example, your

---

[1] Terms in bold are defined in the glossary on the next page.

search engine will retrieve all pages that have the term "school" in them. Some of these pages will certainly describe specific schools, but others may include a description of someone's education or even schools of fish! If your search term is more than one word, you must put quotation marks around the entire term so that the search tool treats it as a single search item. If you don't enclose it in quotation marks, the search engine will look for each of those words separately and you'll end up with a lot of useless information. For instance, typing *Job Lane School* without quotation marks in an English text field would retrieve *all* pages relating to jobs, lanes, or schools.

No matter which search tool you use, you will eventually end up with a results page that has links to different Web sites that might or might not contain the information you are looking for. Often there is a short summary of the contents of the site. Scan these summaries, and choose the sites that you think will be most useful. If the results don't fit on one page, click on the link "next" at the bottom of the page.

You can also do more sophisticated searches than those described here. Although each search tool works slightly differently, the basic techniques for using them are fairly consistent. You can learn how each search tool can help you do more effective searches by clicking on terms like "help" or "advanced search."

Make sure you evaluate any sites you find to determine whether they are factual and complete. One way is to check several sites on the same topic or to check the information in a reputable print source, such as an encyclopedia.

Glossary of Web Search Terms

ADDRESS   See **URL**.

BEGIN or **GO BUTTON**   Appears next to a **pulldown menu** or **search term** box on a page. Clicking on it initiates the next action.

BOOKMARK   Used to save a **Web site** address you want to return to. Click and hold on the bookmark menu and then choose "add bookmark." The names of other addresses you have saved will also appear in this menu.

BROWSE   The act of moving through the **WWW** by means of **links**.

BROWSER   A software application that allows you to access the resources of the **WWW**. Netscape Navigator and Internet Explorer are examples of browsers.

CLICK   The action of depressing a mouse button while the **pointer** is pointing at a specific object.

GO BUTTON   See **begin button**.

HOMEPAGE   A page that a user or organization has designated as the first page of its **Web site**.

HOT SPOTS   Graphics or areas of graphics that allow you to **click** on a **link** that corresponds to the graphic.

INTERNET   A vast, worldwide network of computers and related networks that are able to communicate with each other by means of common standards.

KEYWORD   See **search term**.

LINK Words or graphics that allow you to move within a document or to another document on the **Internet**. Text links are often indicated by words that are highlighted in a different color and/or underlined. Graphic links are sometimes outlined in a contrasting color. Links can always be identified by the way your **pointer** changes as you pass over them. Also known as "hyperlink."

LOCATION BOX Contains the **URL** of the page that you are looking at. This is the information that you will need to note to locate a page again quickly, or you can **bookmark** it.

NAVIGATION Similar to **browsing,** but is usually more focused.

NET Short for **Internet.**

NET SEARCH BUTTON A button on the **toolbar** that accesses a variety of **search tools.**

PAGE Document on the **WWW**; also referred to as **Web page**.

PATH The route one follows to arrive at a list of **Web sites** when using a **Web guide**.

POINTER Associated with movement of your mouse. It changes shape for different functions that are defined by the software program you are using. Common functions are an arrow to indicate where you are on a screen, a hand to indicate a **link,** and an I-bar to indicate that you can enter text.

PULLDOWN MENU Shows the options associated with that menu. **Scrolling** to the desired option and releasing the mouse selects the option. The resulting action may occur automatically or you may need to click on a **go, begin,** or **start button.**

SCROLL The act of moving through an electronic document.

SCROLL BARS Bars at the edges of a document that allow you to move through the document.

SEARCH BUTTON Similar to the **begin button,** a button that initiates a search.

SEARCH ENGINE A program that works with your **browser** to find information on the **Web.**

SEARCH TERM The word or phrase you use to find specific content in a **search engine** or **Web catalog.**

SEARCH TOOL A **search engine** (such as Alta Vista) or **Web guide** (such as Yahoo!).

START BUTTON See **begin button.**

SURF See **browse.**

TOOLBAR Graphics and/or text at the top of a **browser** that allow you to initiate certain functions by clicking on the graphics or text.

TEXT FIELD The area in which you type in text on-screen. For example, the place you type in your **search term** in a **search engine**.

URL Short for Uniform Resource Locator, and sometimes known as an **address.** URLs are used for identifying all content on the **WWW.**

WEB Short for **World Wide Web.**

WEB CATALOG See **Web guide.**

WEB GUIDE A database of **Web pages** and other materials on the **Web.** These pages and materials are reviewed regularly for their usefulness and appropriateness to the subject heading used in the catalog.

WEB PAGE A document on the **WWW**, often containing text and graphics.

WEB SITE A collection of related **Web pages** in a single location connected by **links.**

WORLD WIDE WEB A part of the **Internet** that allows users to exchange information using text, graphics, sound, animation, and video.

WWW Short for **World Wide Web.**

French-Speaking Countries and Regions and Monetary Unit Chart

Country or Region	Capital	Monetary Unit
L'Europe		
l'Union *(f.)* européenne	——	euro
la Belgique	Bruxelles	Belgian franc
la France	Paris	French franc
le Luxembourg	Luxembourg	Luxembourg franc
la Suisse	Berne	Swiss franc
L'Amérique		
le Canada	Ottawa (Ontario)	Canadian dollar
le Québec	Québec	Canadian dollar
la Louisiane	la Nouvelle-Orléans	U.S. dollar
la Guadeloupe	Basse-Terre	French franc
Haïti *(m.)*	Port-au-Prince	gourde
la Martinique	Fort-de-France	French franc
Saint-Pierre-et-Miquelon	Saint-Pierre	French franc
la Guyane Française	Cayenne	French franc
L'Afrique		
l'Algérie *(f.)*	Algers	Algerian dinar
le Bénin	Porto-Novo	CFA franc[2]
le Burkina-Faso	Ouagadougou	CFA franc
le Burundi	Bujumbura	Burundi franc
le Cameroun	Yaoundé	CFA franc
le Congo	Brazzaville	CFA franc
la Côte-d'Ivoire	Abidjan	CFA franc
Djibouti	Djibouti	Djibouti franc
le Gabon	Libreville	CFA franc
la Guinée	Conakry	Guinean franc
le Mali	Bamako	CFA franc
la Mauritanie	Nouakchott	ouguiya

[2] **C**ommunauté **f**inancière **a**fricaine. All countries in the French Monetary Area share this currency.

le Maroc	Rabat	dirham
le Niger	Niamey	CFA franc
la République Centrafricaine	Bangui	CFA franc
la République démocratique du Congo[3]	Kinshasa	new zaïre
le Ruanda	Kigali	Rwanda franc
le Sénégal	Dakar	CFA franc
le Tchad	N'Djamena	CFA franc
le Togo	Lomé	CFA franc
la Tunisie	Tunis	Tunisian dinar

L'océan Indien

les Comores (*f.pl.*)	Moroni	CFA/Comorian franc[4]
Madagascar	Antananarivo	Malagasy franc
l'île Maurice	Port-Louis	Mauritian rupee
Mayotte	Dzaoudzi	French franc
la Réunion	Saint-Denis	French franc
les Seychelles	Victoria	rupee

L'océan Pacifique

la Polynésie Française	Papeete	French Pacific franc[5]
la Nouvelle-Calédonie	Nouméa	French Pacific franc
Wallis-et-Futuna	Mata-Utu	French Pacific franc

To calculate the amount of foreign currency in dollars, simply multiply the dollar amount by the current exchange rate. For example, if $1 = 6.2 French francs, then $20 = 124 French francs (20 x 6.2).

[3] Until recently, le Zaïre
[4] The Comorian franc's value is fixed to the French franc at the following rate: .75 Comorian Fr = 1 FFr.
[5] The value of the French Pacific franc is fixed to the French franc at the following rate: 18.18 CFP = 1 FFr.

Explorons le Web!

From a Web guide, type "exchange rates" in quotation marks in the Search Keyword box and click on Search to locate Web sites that provide daily rates of exchange of currencies throughout the world. Once the list of selected sites comes up, review the descriptions and investigate sites that you think will have the exchange rate you require.

Clothing and Accessories

les accessoires *(m. pl.)*   *accessories*
les bottes *(f. pl.)*   *boots*
la casquette   *cap*
la ceinture   *belt*
le chapeau   *hat*
les chaussettes *(f. pl.)*   *socks*
les chaussures *(f. pl.)*   *shoes*
la chemise   *shirt*
le chemisier   *blouse*
la combinaison-pantalon   *jumpsuit*
le col pointes boutonnées   *button-down collar*
la cravate   *tie*
le débardeur   *tank top*
la doudoune   *down jacket*
le jean (ample, large)   *(baggy) jeans*
la jupe   *skirt*
les lunettes (de soleil) *(f. pl.)*   *(sun)glasses*
le maillot de bain   *bathing suit*
le manteau   *coat*
le pantalon   *pants*
le polo   *knit shirt, polo shirt*
le pull   *pullover sweater*
le pull à col roulé   *turtleneck*
la robe (bain-de-soleil)   *(sun)dress*
le sac à main   *handbag*
la salopette   *overalls*
les sandales *(f. pl.)*   *sandals*

le short   *shorts*
le survêtement   *jogging suit*
le sweat capuché   *hooded sweatshirt*
le tee   *T-shirt*
les tennis *(f. pl.)*   *sneakers*
la veste   *jacket*
les vêtements *(m. pl.)* de sport   *casual clothing*

Clothing Descriptions

à carreaux   *checked*
à fleurs   *flowered*
à manches courtes   *short-sleeved*
à manches longues   *long-sleeved*
à pois   *polka dot*
à rayures, rayé(é)   *striped*
au dernier cri   *in the latest style*
aux couleurs vives   *colorful*
le coton   *cotton*
le cuir   *leather*
imprimé(e)   *print*
joli(e)   *pretty*
la laine   *wool*
la soie   *silk*
le velours côtelé   *corduroy*

Expressions

Combien coûte ___?   *How much does ___ cost?*
C'est très chic.   *It's very stylish.*
Est-ce-que ça vous va?   *Does it fit you?*
Oui, ça me va à merveille.   *Yes, it fits me beautifully.*

Size Conversion Chart[6]

Men's Suits

U.S	36	38	40	42	44	46
Europe	46	48	51	54	56	58

Men's Shirts

U.S.	14	14.5	15	15.5	16	16.5
Europe	36	37	38	39	40	41

[6] These are approximate conversions. There are variations among countries.

Women's Dresses, Coats, Blouses					
U.S.	6	8	10	12	14	16
Europe	36	38	40	42	44	46

Women's Shoes								
U.S.	6	6.5	7	7.5	8	8.5	9	9.5	10
Europe	37	38	38	39	39	40	40	41	41

Men's Shoes									
U.S.	7.5	8	8.5	9	9.5	10	10.5	11	11.5	12
Europe	41	41	42	43	43	44	44	45	45	46

Clubs and Organizations

le club d'allemand   *German club*
le club de débat   *debating club*
le club de drame   *drama club*
le club d'échecs   *chess club*
le club d'espagnol   *Spanish club*
le club de français   *French club*
le club de lettres   *literary magazine*

le club de maths   *math club*
le club de photographie   *photography club*
le club de science   *science club*
le club de ski   *ski club*
le gouvernement des étudiants   *student government*
la liste d'honneur   *honor society*

Colors

argenté(e)   *silver*
blanc (blanche)   *white*
blanc uni   *solid white*
bleu(e)   *blue*
bleu clair   *light blue*
bleu marine   *navy blue*
bordeaux   *maroon*
brun(e)   *brown*
gris(e)   *gray*

jaune   *yellow*
noir(e)   *black*
orange   *orange*
rose   *pink*
rouge   *red*
vert(e)   *green*
vert foncé   *dark green*
violet(te)   *purple*

Food and Nutrition

l'abricot *(m.)*   *apricot*
l'ananas *(m.)*   *pineapple*
la banane   *banana*
le café (au lait)   *coffee (with hot milk)*
la carotte   *carrot*
la cerise   *cherry*
la confiture   *jam*
les céréales *(f. pl.)*   *(breakfast) cereal*

le croissant   *croissant*
les farineux *(m. pl.)*   *carbohydrates*
la fraise   *strawberry*
les frites *(f. pl.)*   *French fries*
le fromage   *cheese*
le fruit   *fruit*
le gâteau   *cake*
la glace   *ice cream*

le hamburger   *hamburger*
les haricots verts *(m. pl.)*   *green beans*
le hot dog   *hot dog*
l'huile *(f.)*   *oil [for cooking]*
le jambon   *ham*
le jus (d'orange)   *(orange) juice*
le lait   *milk*
les lasagnes *(f. pl.)*   *lasagna*
le légume   *vegetable*
la matière grasse   *fat [from animals, for cook-ing]*
le milk-shake   *milk shake*
le minéral/les minéraux   *mineral/minerals*
l'œuf *(m.)*   *egg*
l'orange *(f.)*   *orange*
le pain   *bread*
la pamplemousse   *grapefruit*
la pêche   *peach*
les petits pois *(m. pl.)*   *peas*
la pizza   *pizza*
le poisson   *fish*
la pomme   *apple*
la pomme de terre   *potato*
le popcorn   *popcorn*

le poulet   *chicken*
les produits laitiers *(m. pl.)*   *dairy products*
les produits périssables *(m. pl.)*   *perishable foods*
les produits surgelés *(m. pl.)*   *frozen foods*
la protéine   *protein*
le raisin   *grape*
le raisin sec   *raisin*
le riz (frit)   *(fried) rice*
la salade (de thon)   *(tuna) salad*
le sandwich (au beurre de cacahuète et à la confiture)   *(peanut butter and jelly) sandwich*
la sauce   *gravy*
la soupe   *soup*
les spaghettis *(m. pl.)*   *spaghetti*
le sucre   *sugar*
les sucreries *(f. pl.)*   *sweets*
la tarte   *pie*
le taco   *taco*
le thé (glacé)   *(iced) tea*
végétarien(ne) *(adj.)*   *vegetarian*
la viande   *meat*
la vitamine   *vitamin*

Expressions

à point   *medium*
avec modération   *very little, sparingly*
bien cuit   *well done*
saignant   *rare*
Essaie/essayez de manger moins de gras.   *Try to eat less fat.*
Essaie/essayez de manger plus de légumes.   *Try to eat more vegetables.*
Que me recommandez-vous?   *What would you suggest?*

Café Les Jardins
97, avenue des Lilas
Lyon

HORS-D'ŒUVRE
Assiette de crudités $5.95
Escargots à la bourguignonne $6.75

PLATS
Steak au poivre $12.50
Truite aux amandes $10.95
Poulet à la Bresse $9.95

FROMAGES
Plateau de fromages $4.50
Brie, Emmenthal français, Roquefort

BOISSONS
Eau minérale $1.75
Citron pressé $2.25
Café, Thé $.75

DESSERTS
Tartes aux fruits $3.50
Crème caramel $4.50

(Prices in US$)   Service compris

Food Stores

la boucherie   *butcher*
la boulangerie   *bakery*
la crémerie   *dairy store*
l'épicerie *(f.)*   *grocery store*
le marché en plein air   *open-air market*

la pâtisserie   *pastry shop*
la poissonerie   *fish market*
le vendeur/la vendeuse   *salesman/ saleswoman, vendor*

Expressions

Je voudrais un kilo de/d'___, s'il vous plaît. *I'd like a kilo(gram) of ___ please.*
une livre de/d'___ *a pound of ___*
Combien je vous dois? *How much do I owe you?*
Ça fait ___. *That costs ___.*
Je dois faire les courses. *I need to run errands.*

Furniture and Furnishings

Les meubles *(furniture)*

la berceuse *rocking chair*
le bureau *desk*
le canapé *couch*
la chaise (pliante) *(folding) chair*
la commode *chest of drawers*
l'étagère *(f.) bookcase*
le fauteuil *armchair*
le lit (jumeau) *(twin) bed*
le lit de deux personnes *double bed*
les lits superposés *(m. pl.) bunk beds*
le pouf *footstool*
la table *table*
la table de nuit *nightstand*

Le mobilier *(furnishings)*

l'affiche *(f.) poster*
carrelé(e) *(adj.) tiled [of floor, walls, room]*
la chaîne stéréo *stereo system*
le couvre-lit *bedspread*
l'édredon *(m.) comforter*
le lecteur CD *CD player*
la lampe (d'architecte/de bureau)
   (adjustable/desk) lamp
la magnétophone *tape recorder*

le miroir *mirror*
l'oreiller *(m.) pillow*
le papier peint *wallpaper*
peint(e) *(adj.) painted [of wall, furniture, room]*
la peinture *picture*
la photo *photo*
la radio *radio*
le rail d'éclairage *track lighting*
les rideaux *(m. pl.) curtains*
le store (vénitien) *shade (Venetian blind)*
le tapis *rug*
la télé *television*
le téléphone *telephone*
peindre *to paint*
tapisser *to wallpaper; to carpet*

Les parties d'une pièce *(parts of a room)*

la fenêtre *window*
le mur *wall*
le placard *closet*
le plafond *ceiling*
le plancher *floor*
la porte *door*

Expressions

Amusez-vous comme décorateurs interieurs! *Have fun as interior decorators!*
Nous allons peindre ___ en ___. *We're going to paint [object] in [color].*
Nous allons tapisser les murs. *We're going to wallpaper the walls.*

Holidays

la célébration   *celebration*
célébrer   *to celebrate*
la cérémonie   *ceremony*
la chanson   *song*
civil(e) *(adj.)*   *civil, legal*
commémorer   *to commemorate*
la coutume   *tradition*
le défilé   *parade*
le drapeau   *flag*
les festivités *(f. pl)*   *festivities*
la fête nationale   *national holiday*
les feux d'artifice *(m. pl.)*   *fireworks*
la fleur   *flower*
historique *(adj.)*   *historic*
l'hymne (national) *(m.)*   *(national) anthem*
le jour férié   *legal holiday*

militaire *(adj.)*   *military*
la musique   *music*
politique *(adj.)*   *political*
religieux/religieuse *(adj.)*   *religious*
le symbole   *symbol*
la tradition   *tradition*

Some Holidays

Hanoukka *(f.)*   *Hannukah*
la fête du Travail *(May 1)*   *Labor Day*
le jour de l'an   *New Year's Day*
Mardi gras   *Mardi Gras*
Noël   *Christmas*
pâque *(f.)*   *Passover*
Pâques *(m.)*   *Easter*
le Ramadan   *Ramadan*

Musical Instruments

l'alto *(m.)*   *viola*
le basson   *bassoon*
la clarinette   *clarinet*
le clavier   *keyboard*
la contrebasse   *bass*
le cor   *horn*
le cor d'harmonie   *French horn*
la flûte   *flute*
la guitare   *guitar*

l'harmonica *(m.)*   *harmonica*
le hautbois   *oboe*
le piano   *piano*
le saxo(phone)   *saxophone*
le tambour   *drum*
le trombone   *trombone*
la trompette   *trumpet*
le tuba   *tuba*
le violon   *violin*
le violoncelle   *cello*

Sports and Games

General Terms

l'athlète *(m.)*   *athlete*
être mauvais(e)/bon(ne) perdant(e)   *to be a bad/good loser*
le gagnant/la gagnante   *winner*
gagner   *to win*
la ligne d'arrivée   *finish line*

la ligne de départ   *starting line*
marquer   *to score*
mesurer   *to measure*
le mètre à ruban   *measuring tape*
Où en est le jeu, le match?   *What's the score?*

le perdant/la perdante *loser*
perdre *to lose*
le score *score*
tricher *to cheat*

Sports

l'aérobic *(f.)* *aerobics*
les arts martiaux *(m. pl.)* *martial arts*
l'athlétisme *(m.)* *track*
l'aviron *(m.)* *rowing, crew*
le base-ball *baseball*
le basket *basketball*
l'équitation *(f.)* *horseback riding*
l'escalade *(f.)* *rock climbing*
l'escrime *(f.)* *fencing*
faire des haltères *(m. pl.)* *to do weightlifting*
le football (le foot) *soccer*
le football américain *football*

la golfe *golf*
la gymnastique *gymnastics*
le hockey sur glace *ice hockey*
le hockey sur herbe *field hockey*
la lutte gréco-romaine *wrestling*
la natation *swimming*
le ski *skiing*
le ski du fond *cross-country skiing*
le ski nautique *waterskiing*

Games

le dé/les dés *die/dice*
le jeu de cartes *deck of cards; card game*
la joueur/la joueuse *player*
la pioche *stack/deck of cards to draw from*
le pion *playing piece*
le tableau *game board*
le sablier *timer, hourglass*

Expressions

À toi de jouer. *It's your turn (to play).*
Avance d'/de ___ case(s). *Move ahead ___ space(s).*
À vos marques! *On your mark!*
Prets! *Get set!*
Partez! *Go!*
C'est à qui le tour? *Whose turn is it?*
C'est à moi. *It's mine.*
C'est à [Anne]. *It's [Anne's].*
Comptez! *Count!*
Et si on jouait? *How about playing a game?*
J'ai besoin de deux cartes. *I need two cards.*
Jette les dés. *Roll the dice.*
Mets ton pion sur la case de départ. *Put your piece on the starting space.*
Pioche/tire une carte. *Pick up/draw a card.*
Recule d'/de ___ case(s). *Go back ___ spaces.*
Si tu tombes sur ___, va au/à l'/à la/aux ___. *If you land on ___, go to ___.*
Tu as besoin de combien de cartes? *How many cards do you need?*
Va au/à la/aux ___. *Go to ___.*

Subjects and Courses

les affaires *(f. pl.) business*
l'algèbre *(f.)   algebra*
l'allemand *(m.)   German*
l'anglais *(m.)   English*
les arts *(m. pl.)* ménagers   *home economics*
la biologie   *biology*
le calcul   *calculus*
le chant   *singing, chorus*
la chemie   *chemistry*
la danse   *dance*
le dessin (industriel)   *(technical) drawing*
l'éducation *(f.)* physique et sportive (EPS)
   physical education
l'enseignement *(m.)* industriel   *industrial arts*
l'espagnol *(m.)   Spanish*
le français   *French*
la géométrie   *geometry*
l'histoire *(f.)* américaine   *American history*
l'histoire *(f.)* du monde   *world history*

l'informatique *(f.)   computer science*
le journalisme   *journalism*
le latin   *Latin*
les mathématiques (les maths) *(f. pl.)   math*
la musique   *music*
l'orchestre *(m.)* d'école   *marching band*
la peinture   *painting*
la philosophie   *philosophy*
la physique   *physics*
la psychologie   *psychology*
la réparation d'auto   *car repair*
le russe   *Russian*
la science économique *(f.)   economics*
les sciences *(f. pl.)   science*
la sociologie   *sociology*
le théâtre   *theater/acting*
le traitement de texte   *word processing*
les travaux *(m. pl.)* pratiques   *lab class/*
   discussion group

Weather

Quel temps fait-il?   *What's the weather like?*

Le beau temps *(nice weather)*

de brèves éclaircies *(f. pl.)   brief periods*
   of clearing
un ciel dégagé   *a clear sky*
l'éclaircie *(f.)   sunny spell*
ensoleillé(e) *(adj.)   sunny*
Il fait beau.   *It's nice weather.*
Il fait du soleil.   *It's sunny.*

Les nuages *[m. pl.] (clouds)*

la brume   *fog*
le ciel couvert   *cloudy, overcast*
le nuage chargé de pluie   *rain cloud*
nuageux/nuageuse *(adj.)   cloudy*
peu nuageux   *partly cloudy*
Le ciel est couvert.   *It's cloudy.*

La pluie *(rain)*

l'averse *(f.)* *shower (of rain)*
la bruine *(fine) drizzle*
le déluge *downpour*
la forte averse *heavy shower, downpour*
Il pleut. *It's raining.*
Il pleut à verse. *It's pouring.*
l'inondation *(f.)* *flood*
le mauvais temps *bad weather*
les pluies intermittentes *(f. pl.)* *scattered showers*
Une pluie fine tombe. *It is drizzling.*

L'orage *[m.] (storm, thunderstorm)*

l'avis *(m.)* d'ouragan/de tornade *hurricane/ tornado warning*
une brise légère *breeze, light breeze*
l'éclair *(m., oft. pl.)* *lightning*
Il fait du vent. *It's windy.*
Il fait lourd. *It's muggy, sultry.*

Il fait mauvais. *It's bad weather.*
Il grêle. *It's hailing.*
l'ouragan *(m.)* *hurricane*
la sécheresse *drought*
le tonnerre *thunder*
la tornade *tornado*
le vent *wind*
le vent fort *strong wind*
un vent frais *a strong breeze*

Le froid *(cold weather)*

être bloqué(e) par la neige *to be snowed in*
le givre *frost*
Il neige. *It's snowing.*
la neige *snow*
la neige fondue *sleet*
neigeux/neigeuse *snowy*
la tempête de neige *blizzard*
verglacé(e) *icy*

Temperature: Fahrenheit and Celsius Conversion

As you change temperatures, notice that you are using opposite math operations.

To convert Fahrenheit to **Celsius**, subtract 32 from the Fahrenheit temperature and divide by 1.8.

To convert Celsius to **Fahrenheit**, multiply the Celsius temperature by 1.8 and add 32.

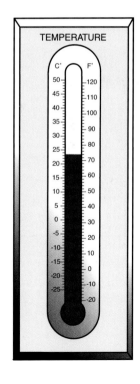

Weights and Measures

Weight

Metric	American/Standard
1 gram	0.03 ounce
1 kilogram (kilo)	2.2 pounds
28 grams	1 ounce
0.45 kilogram	1 pound
900 kilograms	2,000 pounds (1 ton)

Liquid Measure

Metric	American/Standard
1 liter	1.06 quarts
0.47 liter	1 pint
0.95 liter	1 quart
3.8 liters	1 gallon

Distance

Metric	American/Standard
1 meter	39.5 inches (1.1 yards)
1 kilometer	0.62 mile
2.5 centimeters	1 inch
0.3 meter	1 foot
0.9 meter	1 yard
1.6 kilometers	1 mile

Conversion

Multiply **miles** by 1.61 to get **kilometers**

Multiply **kilometers** by 0.62 to get **miles**

Multiply **inches** by 2.54 to get **centimeters**

Multiply **centimeters** by 0.39 to get **inches**

Multiply **feet** by 0.30 to get **meters**

Multiply **meters** by 3.28 to get **feet**

Multiply **yards** by 0.91 to get **meters**

Multiply **meters** by 1.09 to get **yards**

French Equivalents

un centimètre   *centimeter*
un gramme   *gram*
un kilogramme (un kilo)   *kilogram*
un kilomètre   *kilometer*
un litre   *liter*
une livre   *pound*
un mètre   *meter*
un mille   *mile*
une once   *ounce*
un pied   *foot*
une pinte   *pint*
un pouce   *inch*
un quart   *quart*
une tonne   *ton*
un yard   *yard*

METRIC   INCHES

Writing Letters

French speakers usually include the city from where they are writing in front of the date, even in a personal letter.

For the date, use **le** + cardinal number + month (lower case). Exception: For the first of the month, use **1ᵉʳ (premier)**, not **1 (un)**.

In writing to another young person or a very good friend, **Salut** (*Hi!*) is a fine greeting. The most common salutation is **Cher(s)/Chère(s)** (*Dear*). Don't forget to make it agree.

> Chicago, le 21 septembre
>
> Cher Pascal,
>
> Je m'appelle Tom. J'ai 14 ans. Je suis de Chicago, Illinois. J'ai deux frères et un chien (c'est nous sur la photo). J'aime jouer au tennis, lire et nager.
>
> À bientôt!
>
> Tom Pollock

As a sign-off for this letter, **À bientôt!** (*See you soon!*) is a good choice. Use **Amicalement** in most personal letters (*Warmly, Yours truly*) or **Amitiés** (*Best wishes*) for someone you know fairly well.

In writing to someone you are fond of (family or friend), you may sign **Ton (Ta)** + your first name: **Ton James, Ta Caroline.**

> XXX XXXXX
> XXXX XXXXXXX XXXX
> XXXX, XX
> U.S.A
>
> M. Pascal Deschamps
> 127, rue de Rousselet
> 13007 Marseille
> FRANCE

In an international letter, be sure to include your country (U.S.A., Canada) below the city and state or province.

The abbreviation for **Monsieur (M.)** has a period; **Madame** and **Mademoiselle (Mme, Mlle)** have none.

The postal code goes before the city. The country is usually in all caps.

Use a comma after the address number. Note that addresses with **bis** after the number are quite common: **56 bis, rue de Rome (56½).**

Notes

Notes